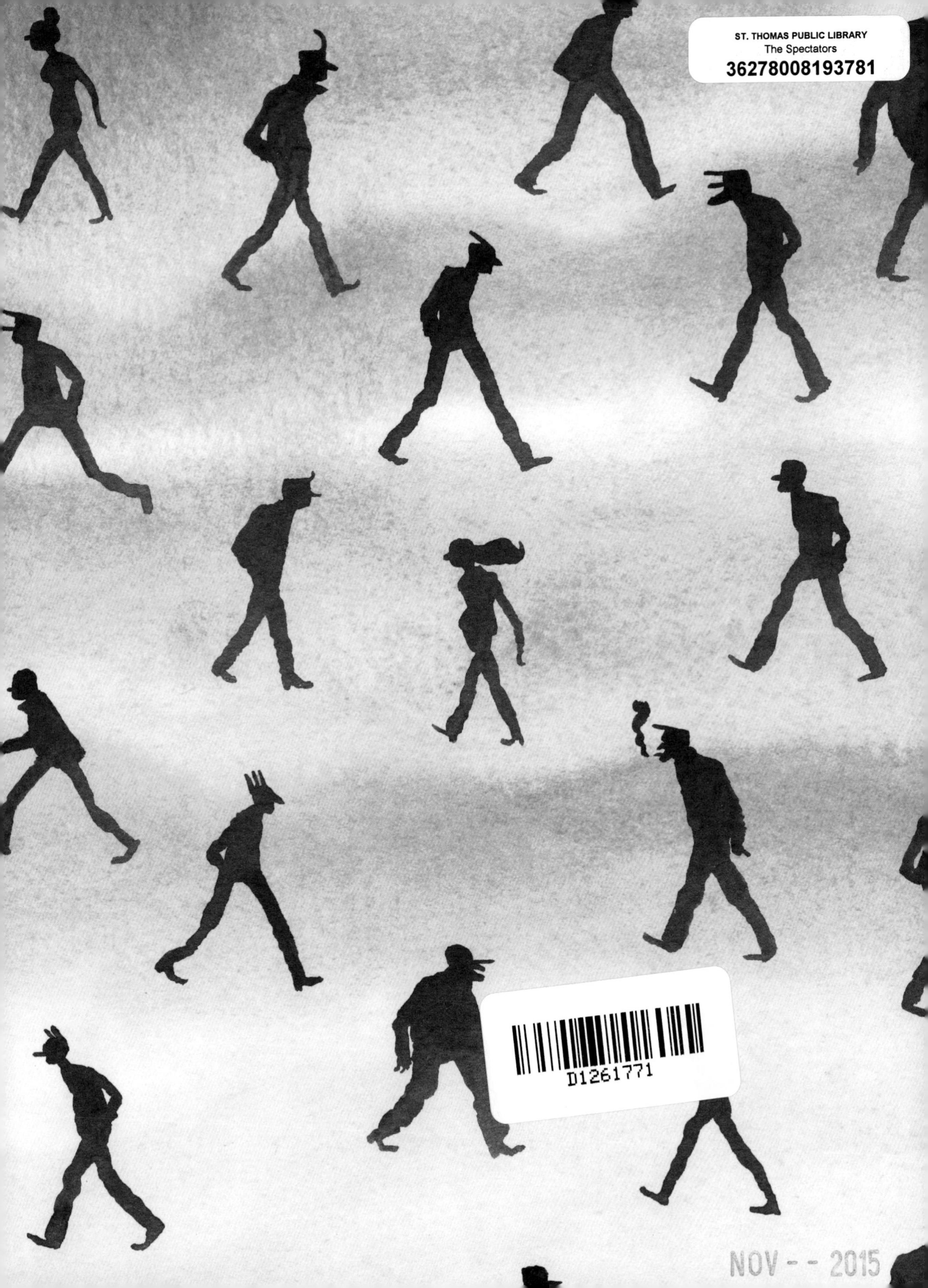

PROLOGUE

Each of us sees the city in our own way.

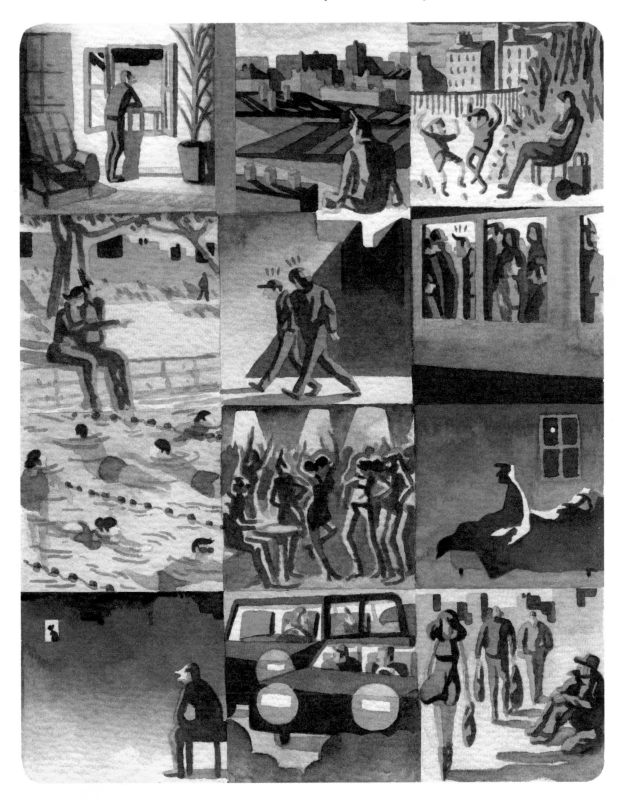

From the rift between sleep and waking bursts of light.

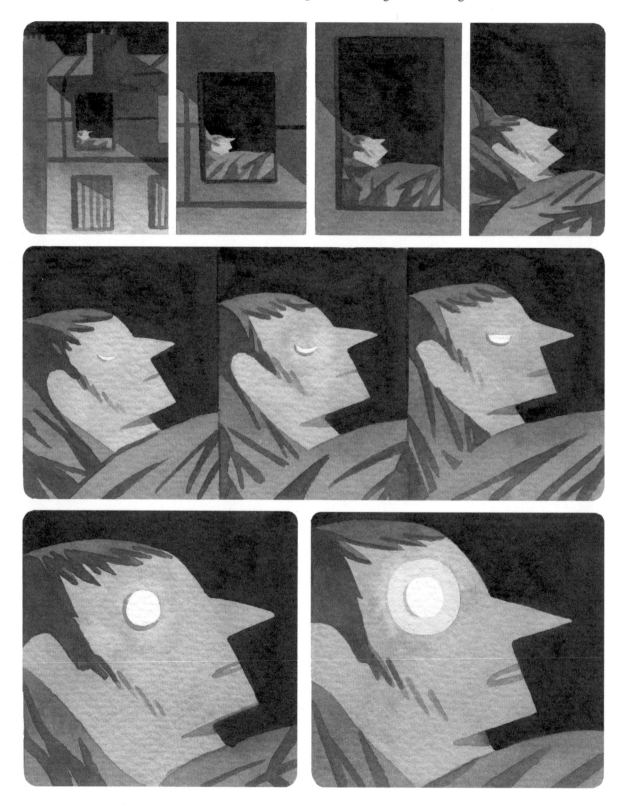

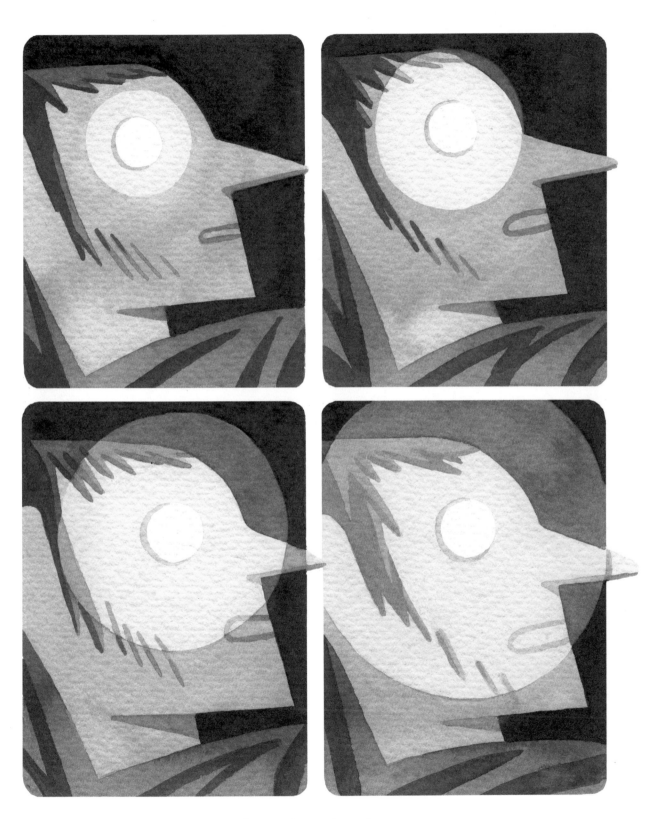

The mind's eye is set free...

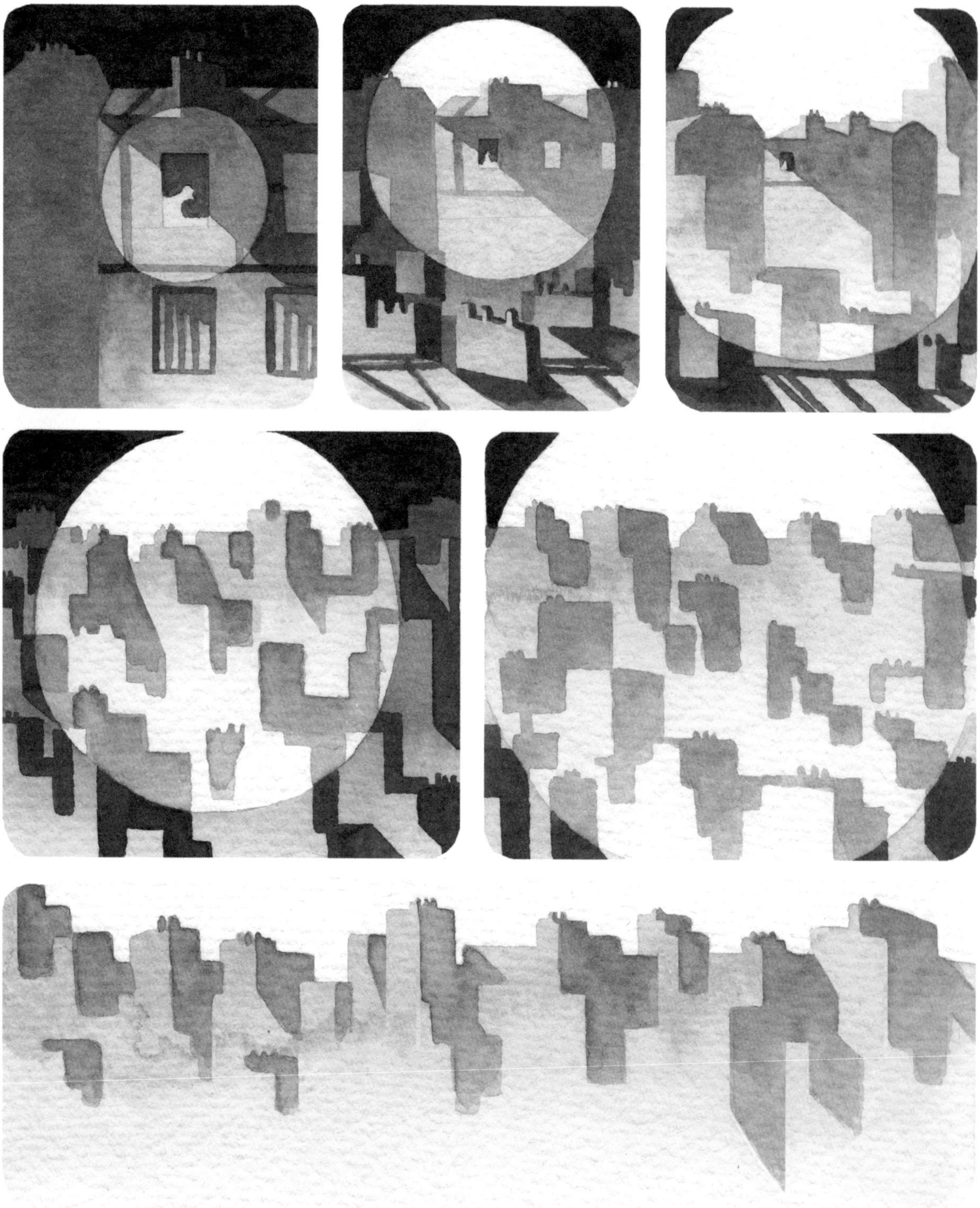

The invisible is revealed.

Thanks to Dominique Detallante.

The Spectators is © Nobrow 2015.

This is a first edition published in 2015 by
Nobrow Ltd. 62 Great Eastern Street, London, EC2A 3QR.

Text and illustrations © Victor Hussenot 2015.
Victor Hussenot has asserted his right under the Copyright, Designs
and Patents Act, 1988, to be identified as the Author of this Work.

Published in the US by Nobrow (US) Inc.

Printed in Poland on FSC assured paper.
ISBN: 978-1-907704-75-8

Order from www.nobrow.net

THE SPECTATORS

Victor Hussenot

NOBROW

London - New York

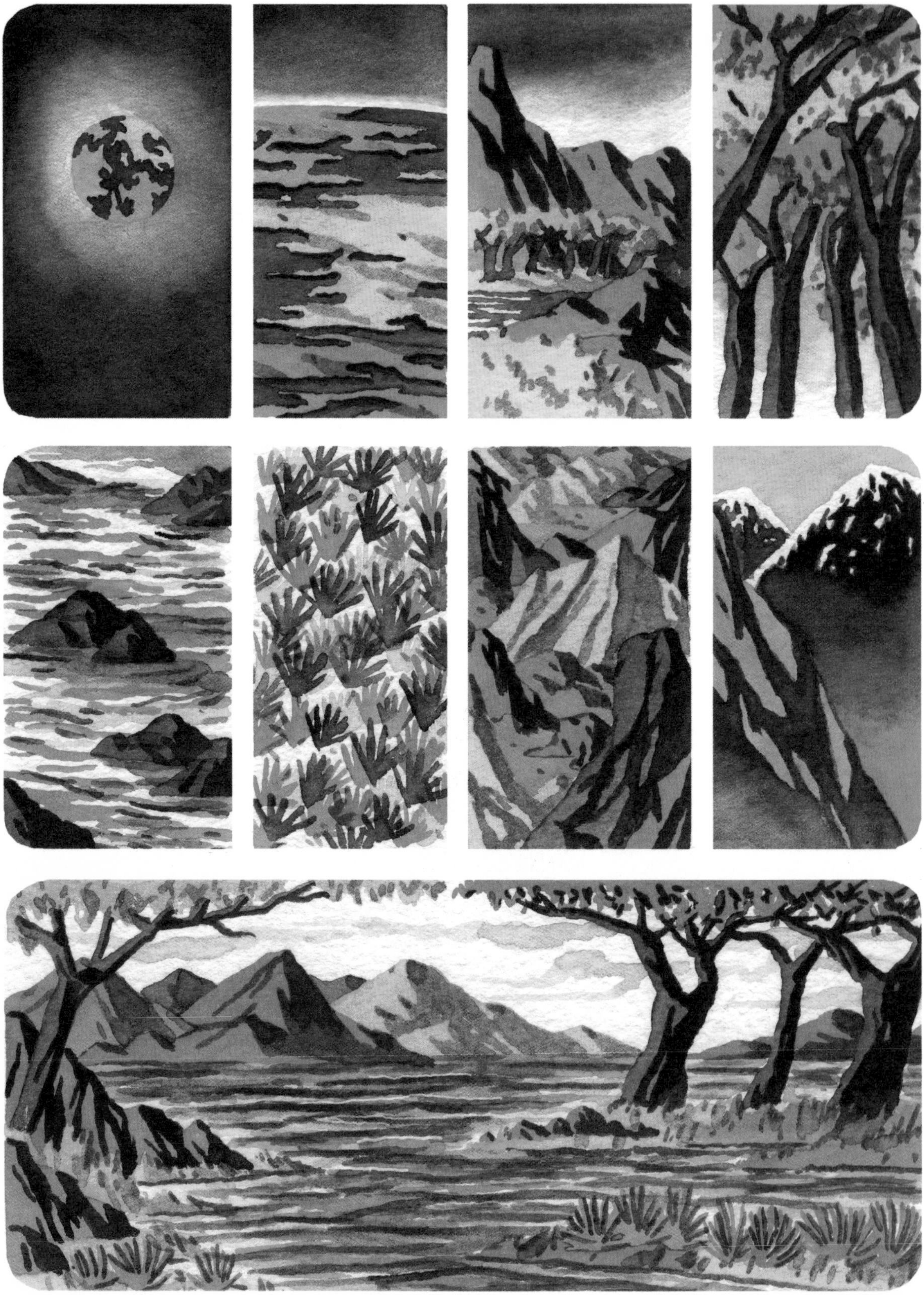

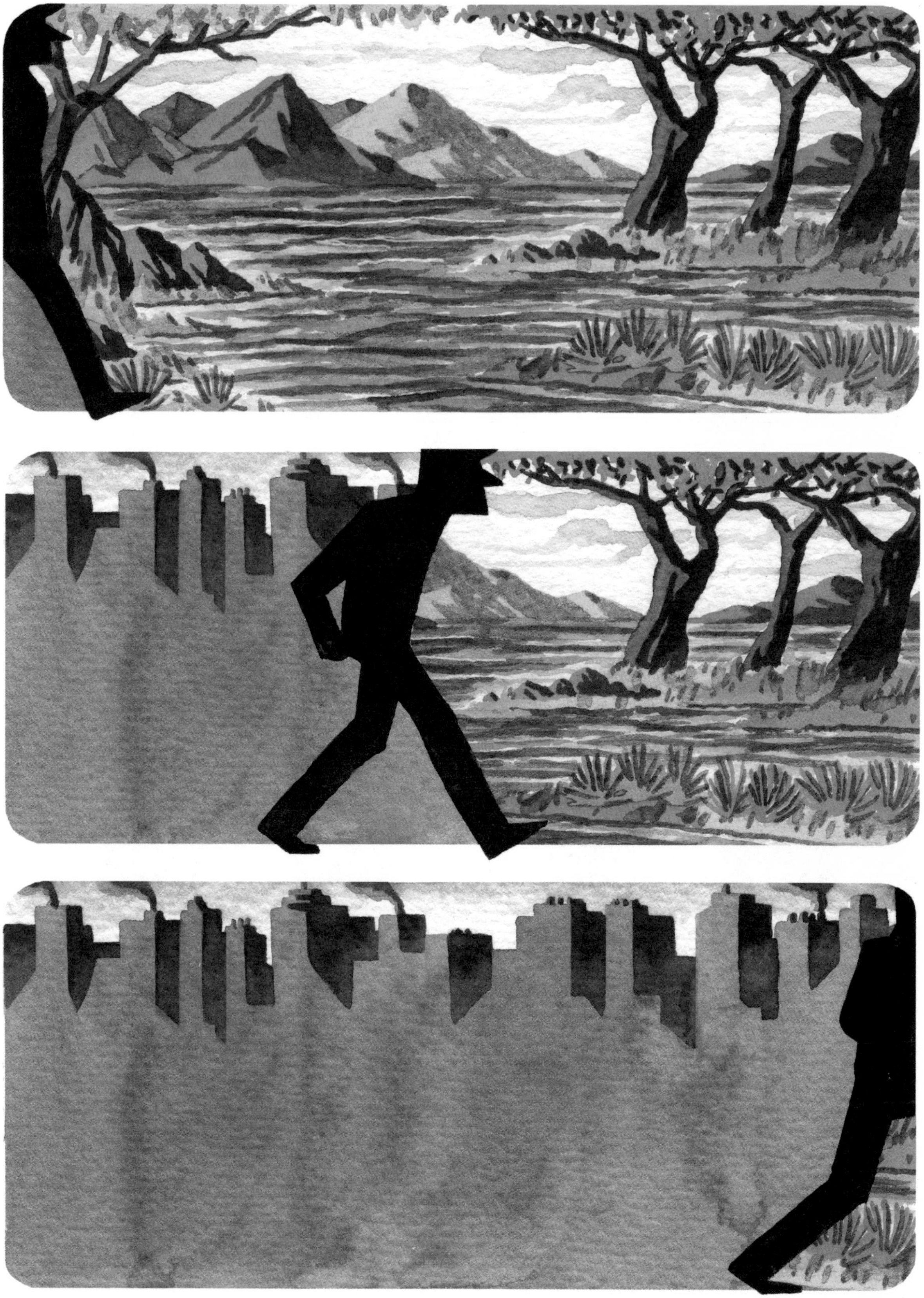

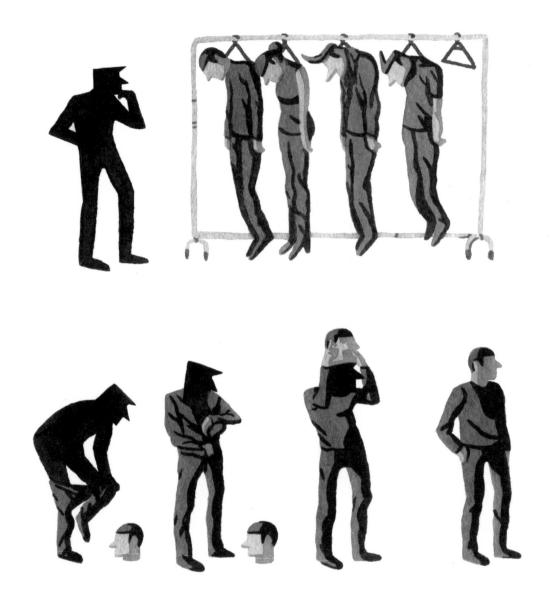

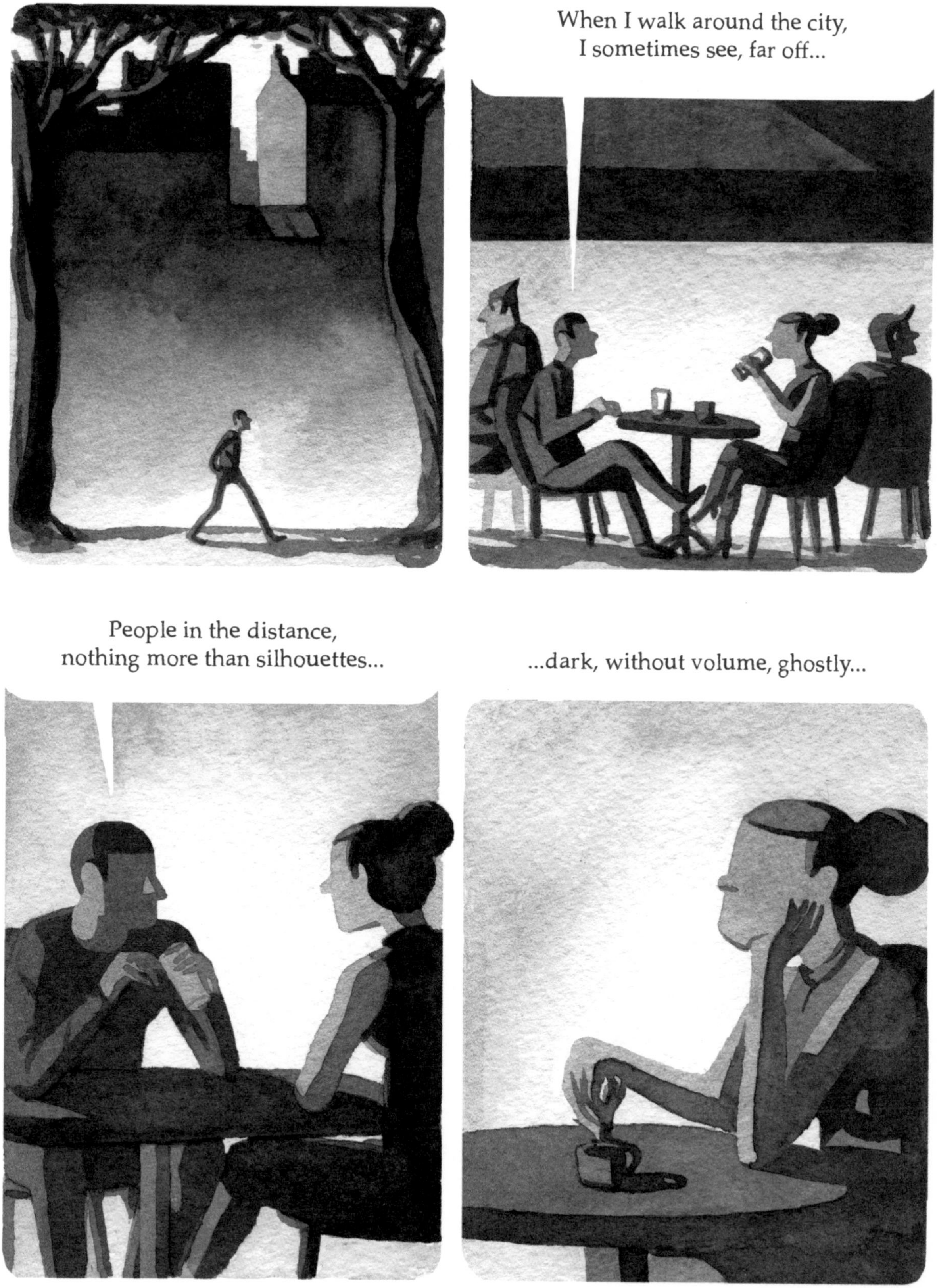
When I walk around the city, I sometimes see, far off...
People in the distance, nothing more than silhouettes...
...dark, without volume, ghostly...

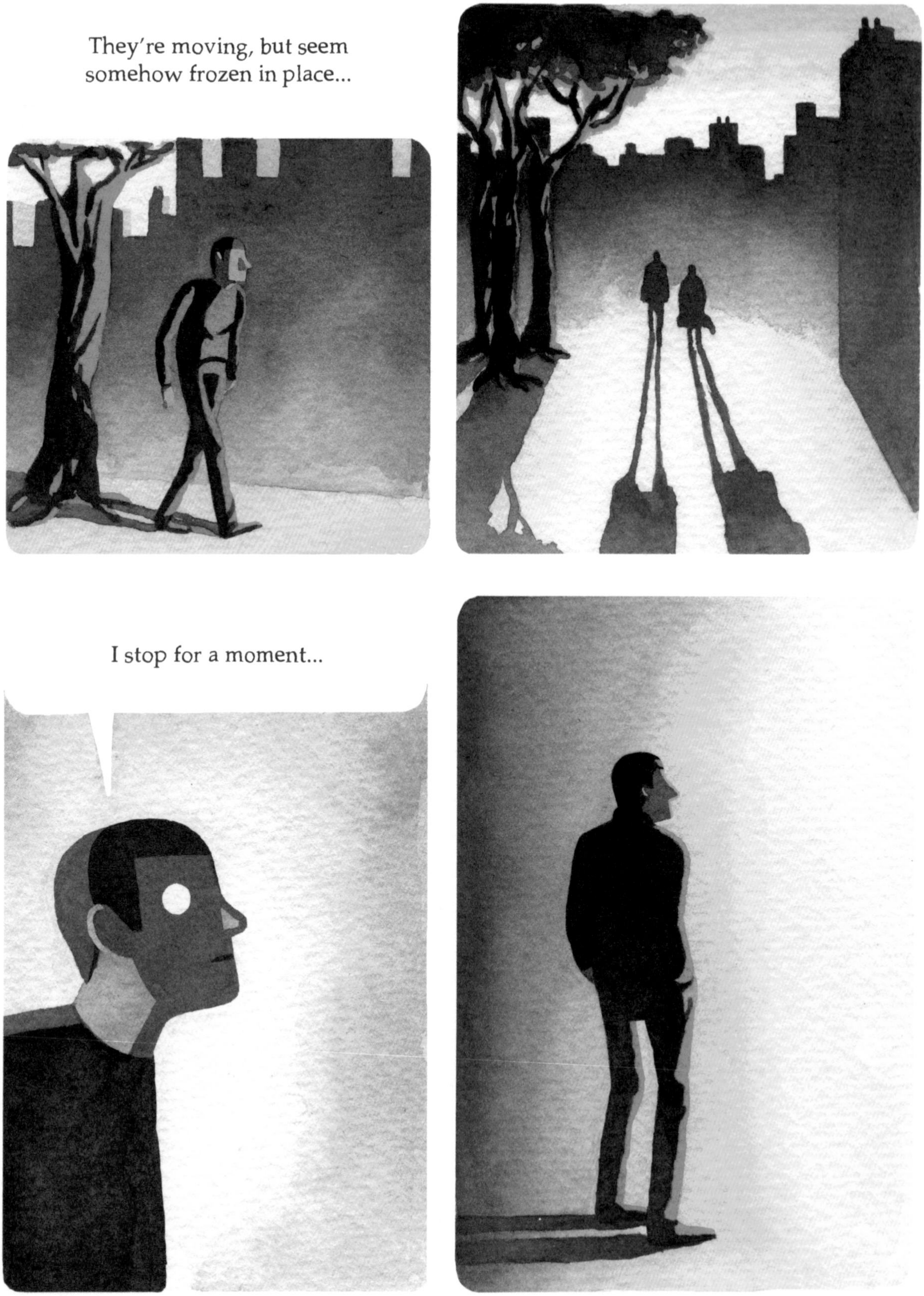
They're moving, but seem somehow frozen in place...
I stop for a moment...

Are they coming closer?
Or moving away? I can't really tell...

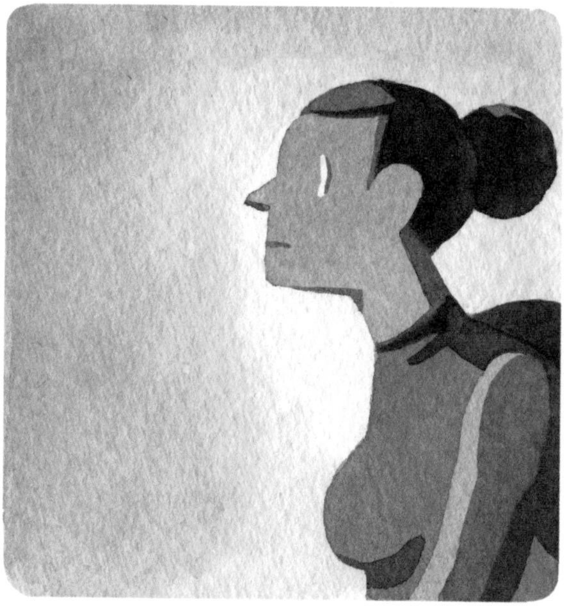

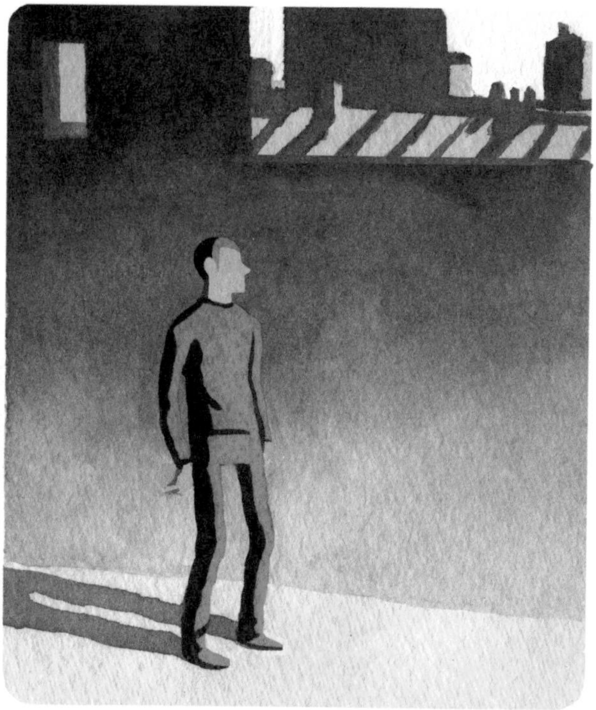

In this moment of grace, they seem freed from time and space.

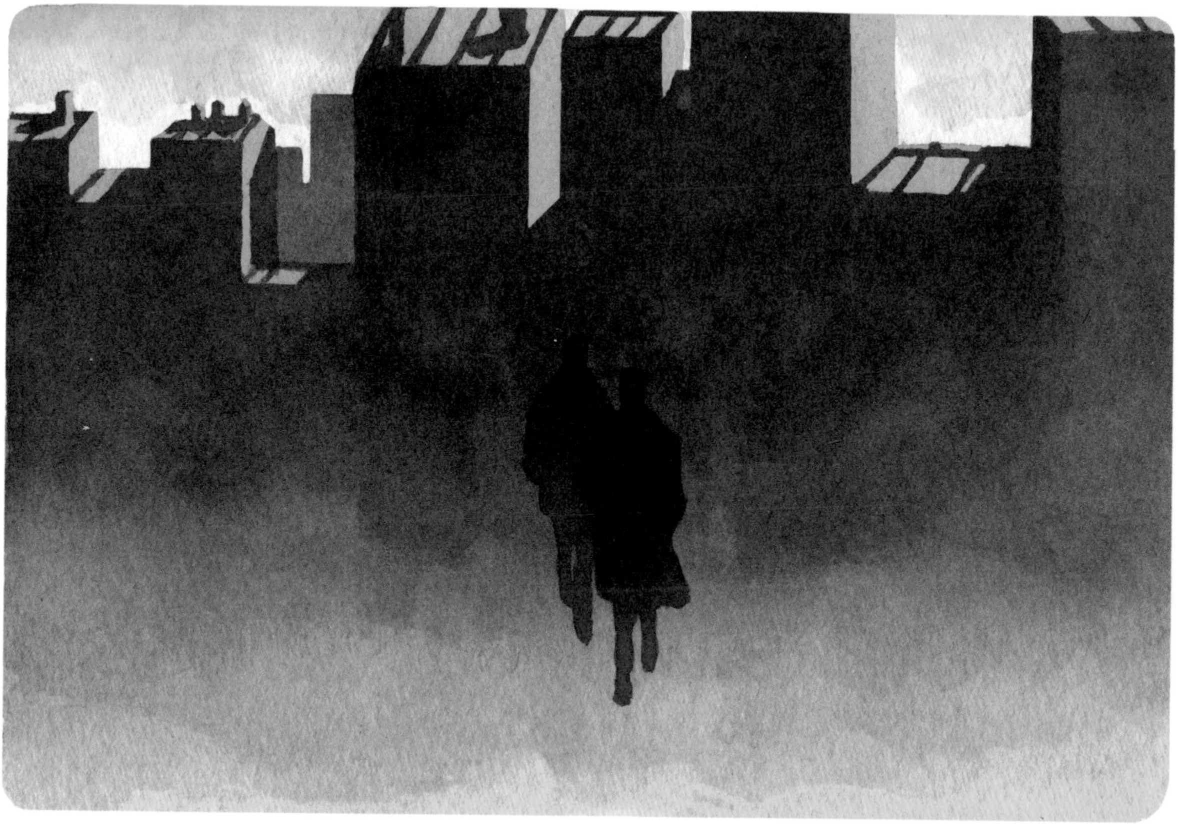

Then, the illusion fades...

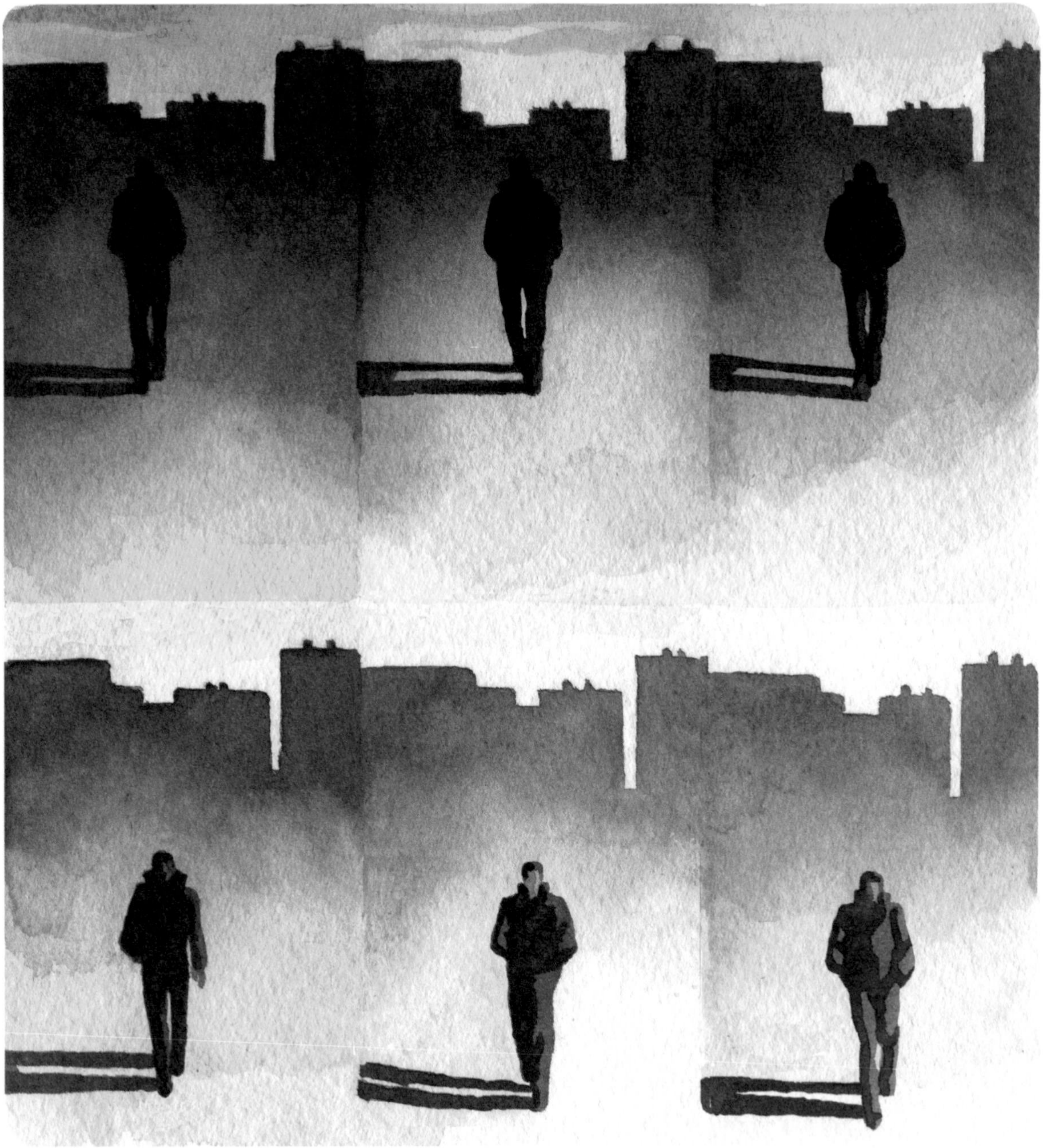

When I revisit certain places,
painful memories resurface:
I find myself back in that moment.

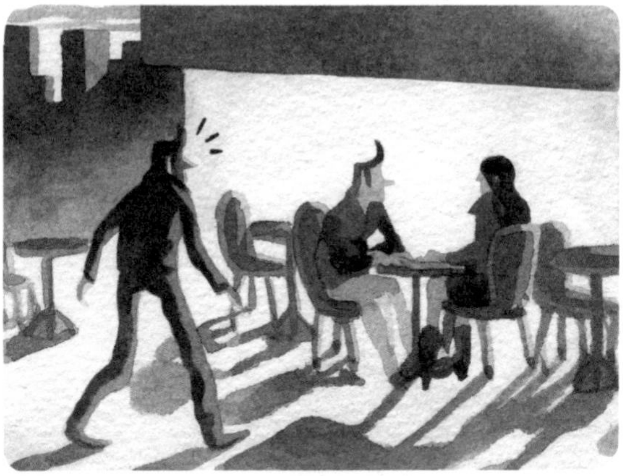

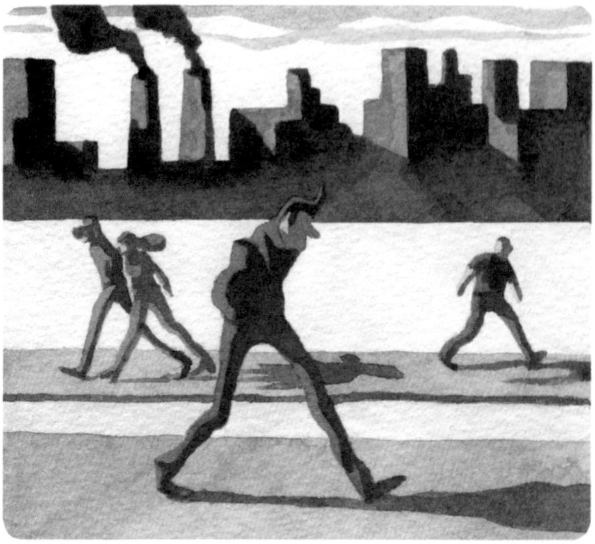

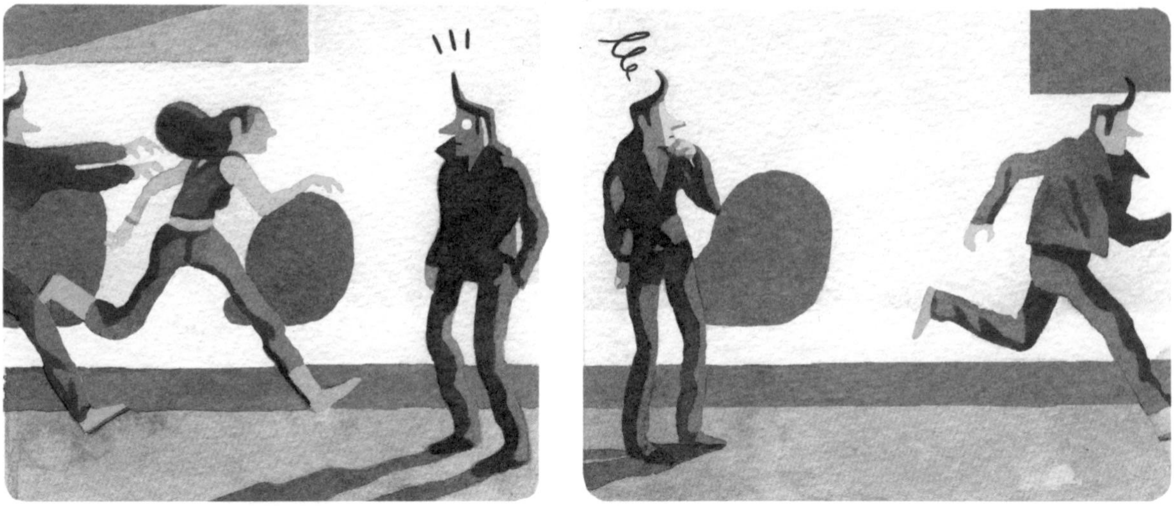

The only way to erase these memories is to return, again and again,
to these same locations and fill them with new moments...

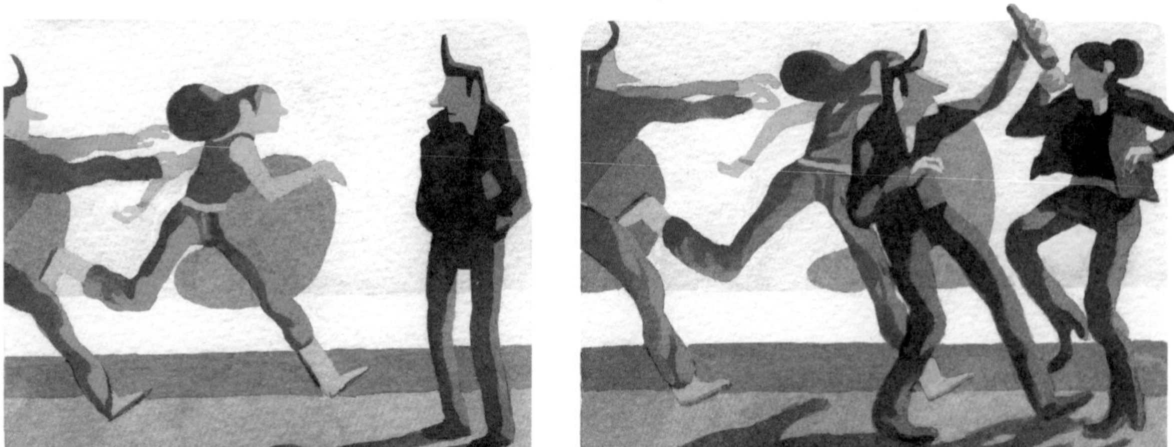

Which in turn will become memories,

which will renew themselves again...

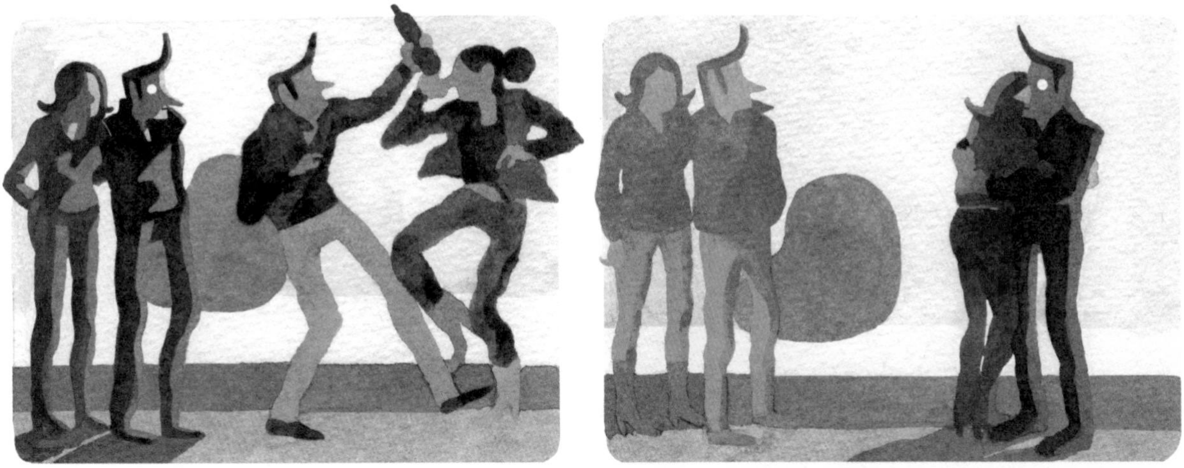

and again...

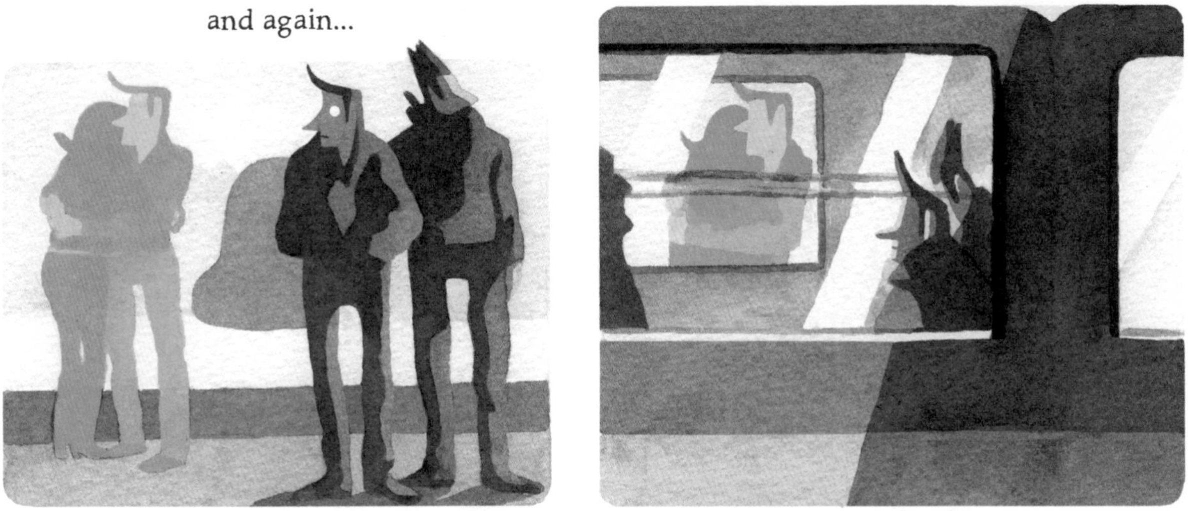

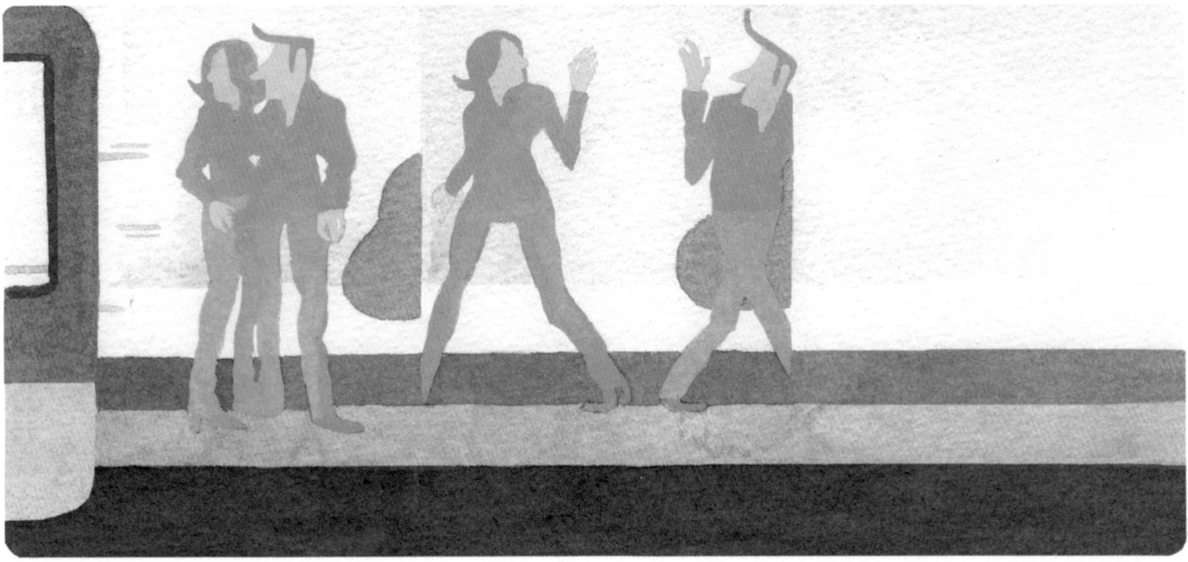

During his nocturnal perambulations, quietly, he observes the city.

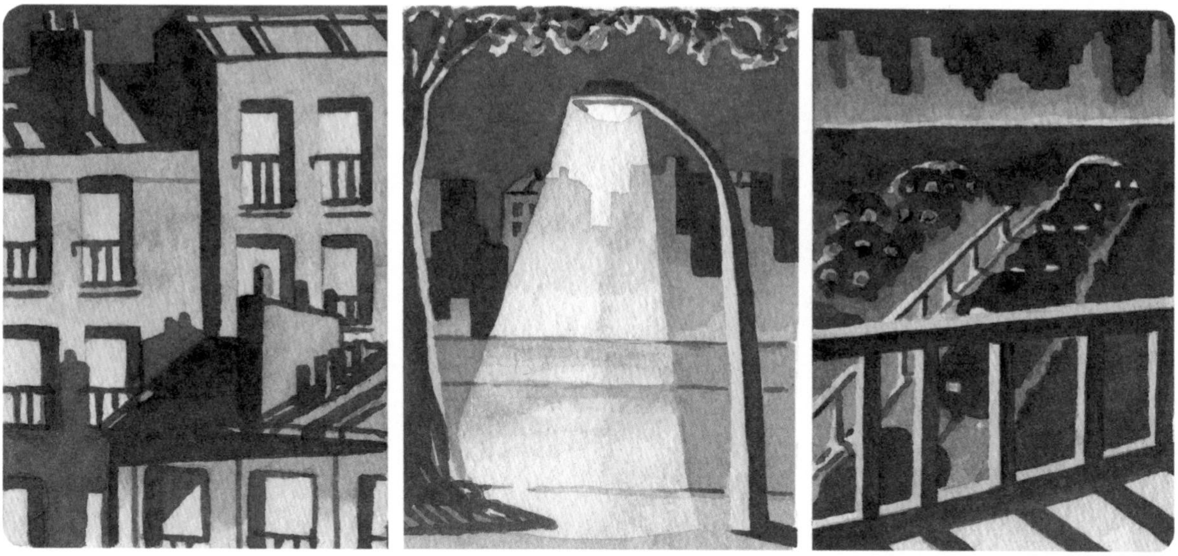

His skin awakens in contact with the air;
the light makes him delirious, and his gaze pierces the landscape...

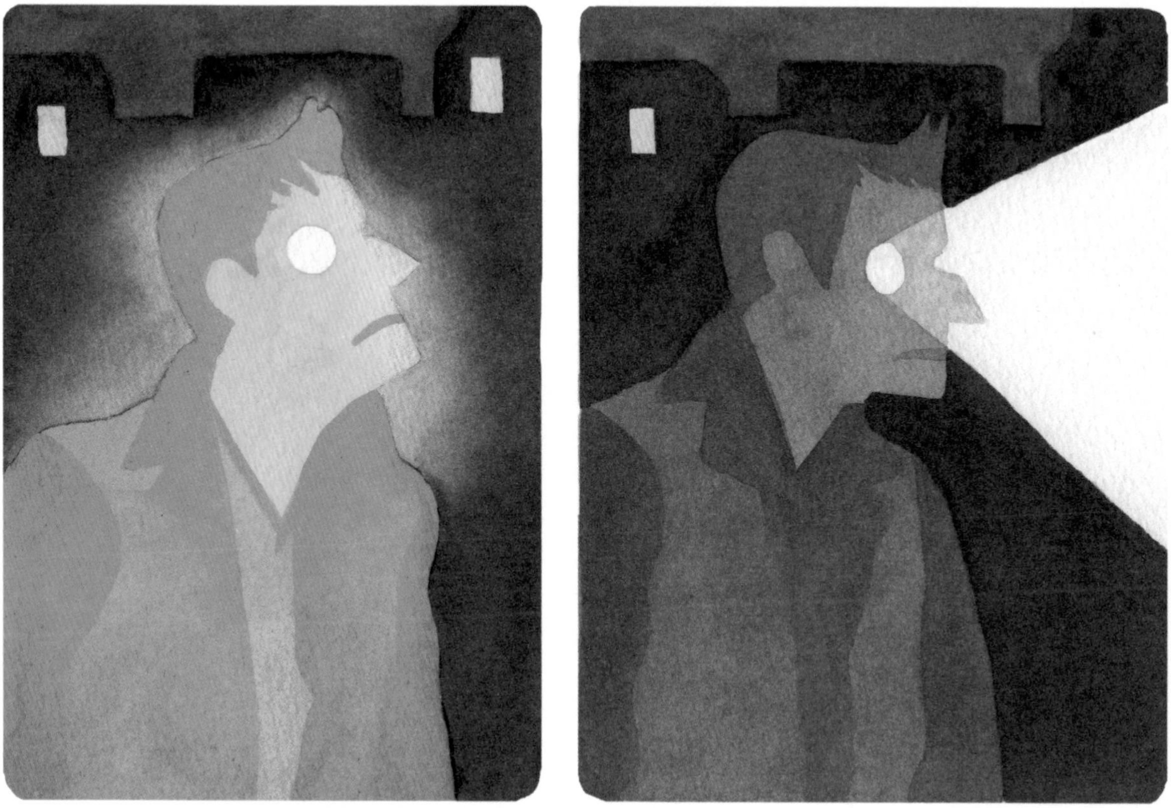

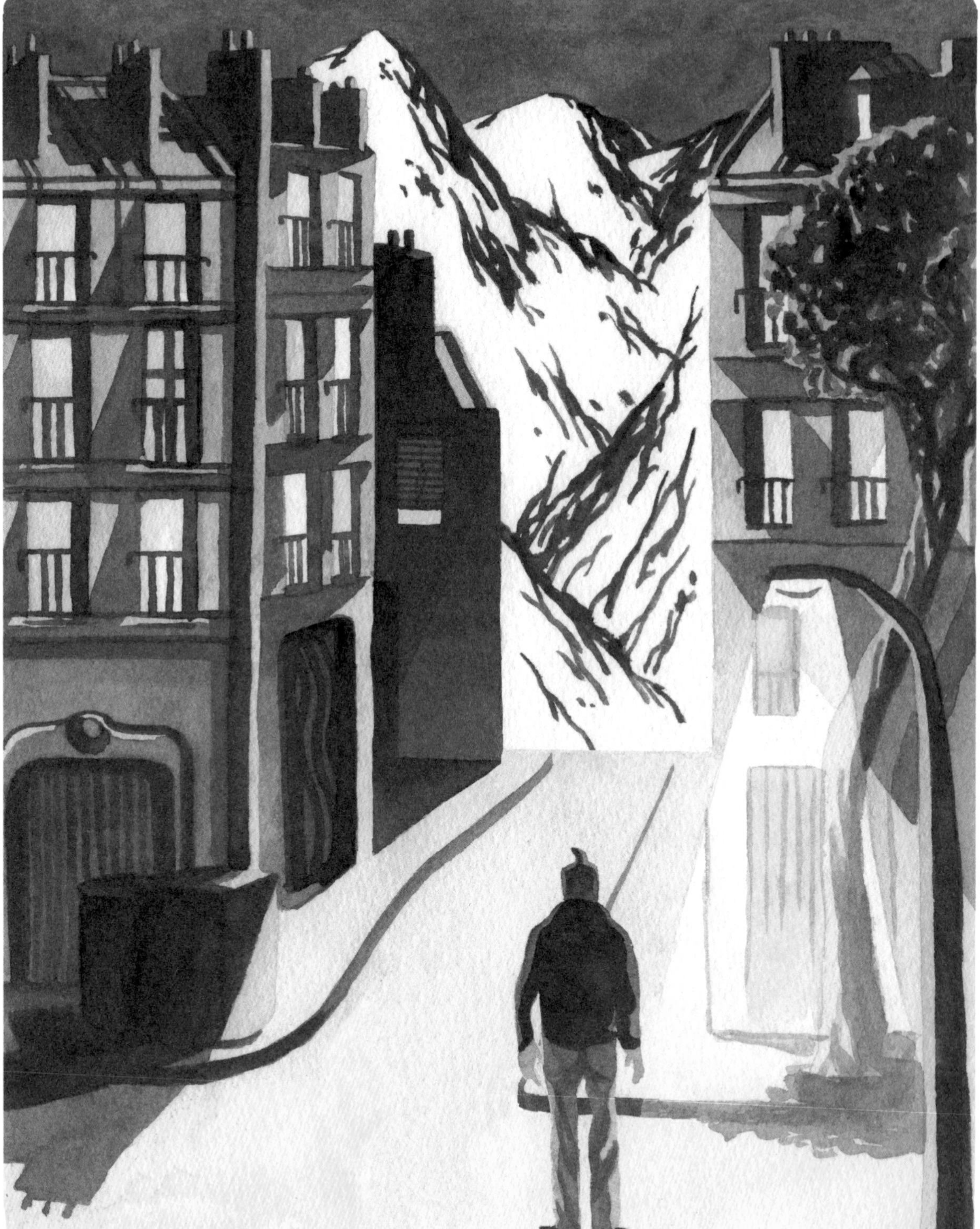

...transforming it.

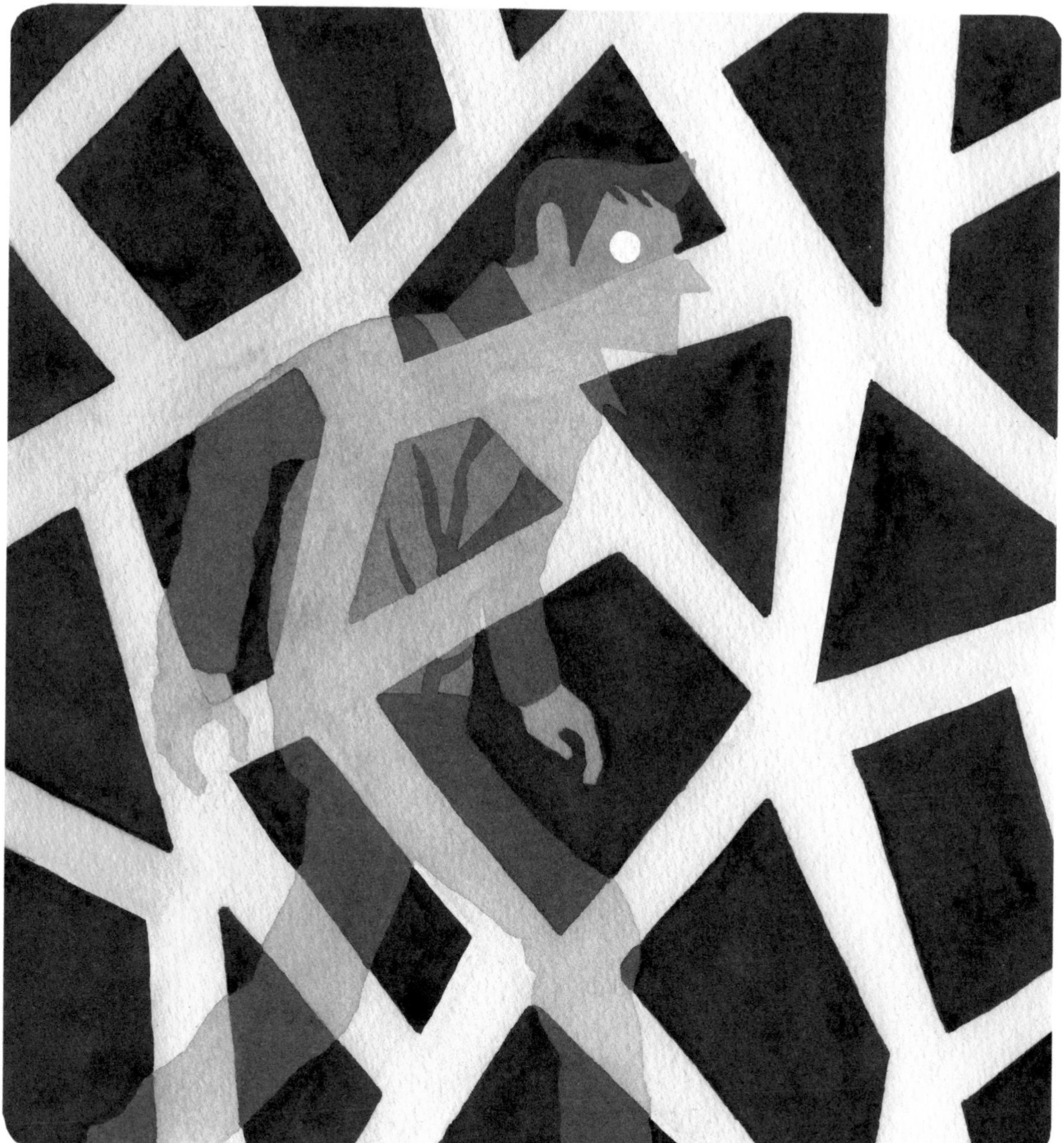

As if drawn by the beam of a lighthouse at sea, he enters a dark tunnel.
When suddenly the lights flare up...

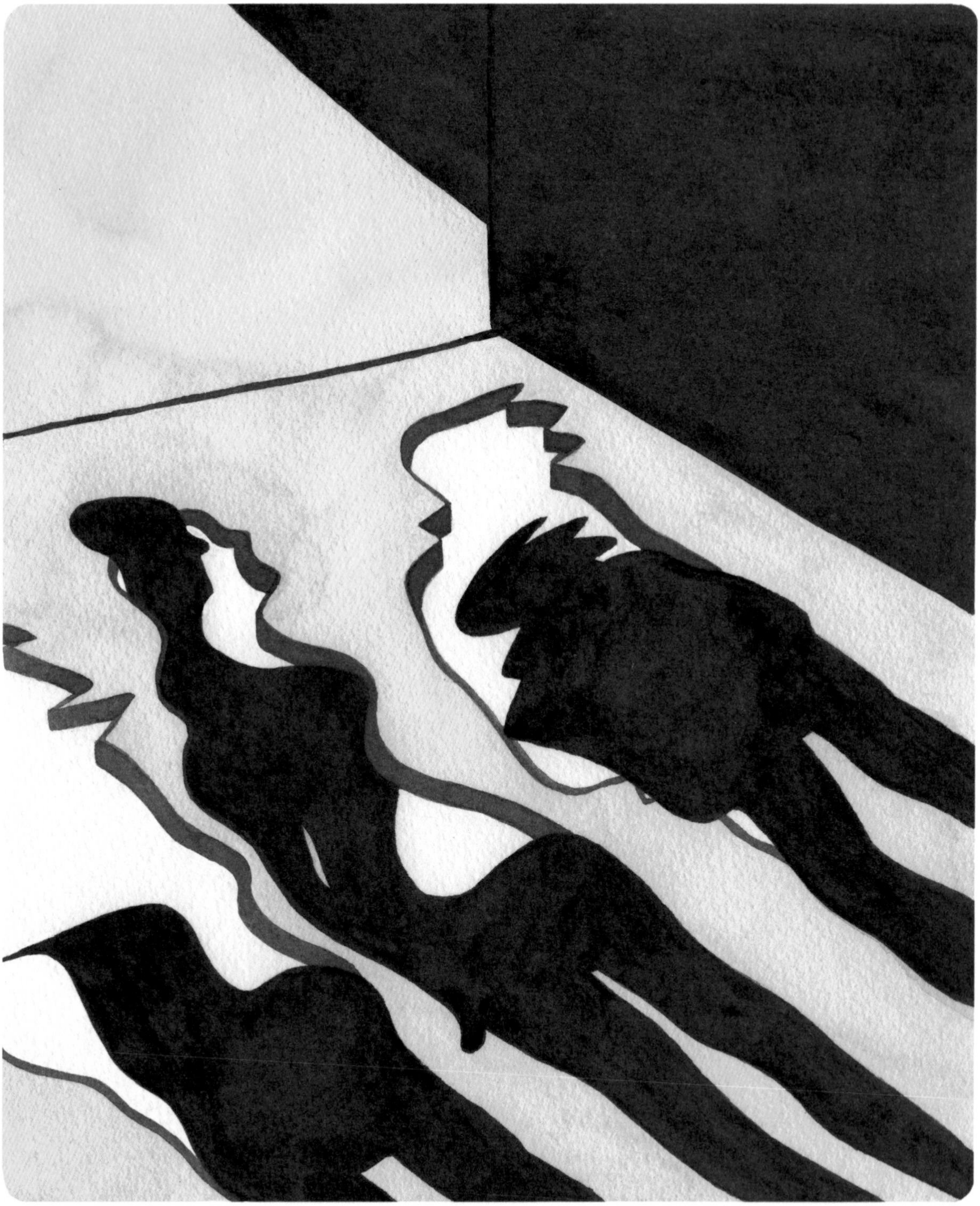

The shadows come to life...

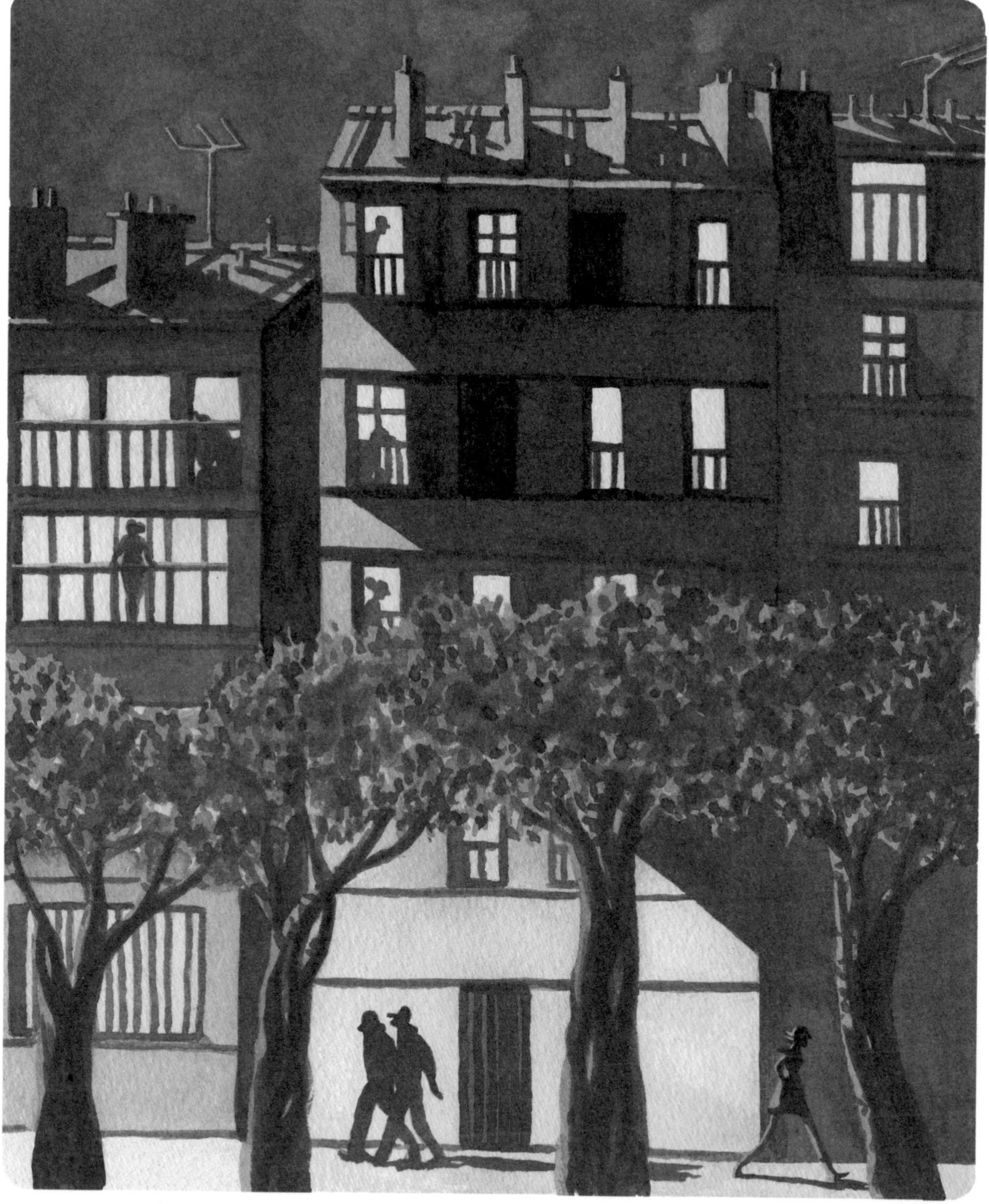

Or play hide-and-seek behind the buildings' facades.

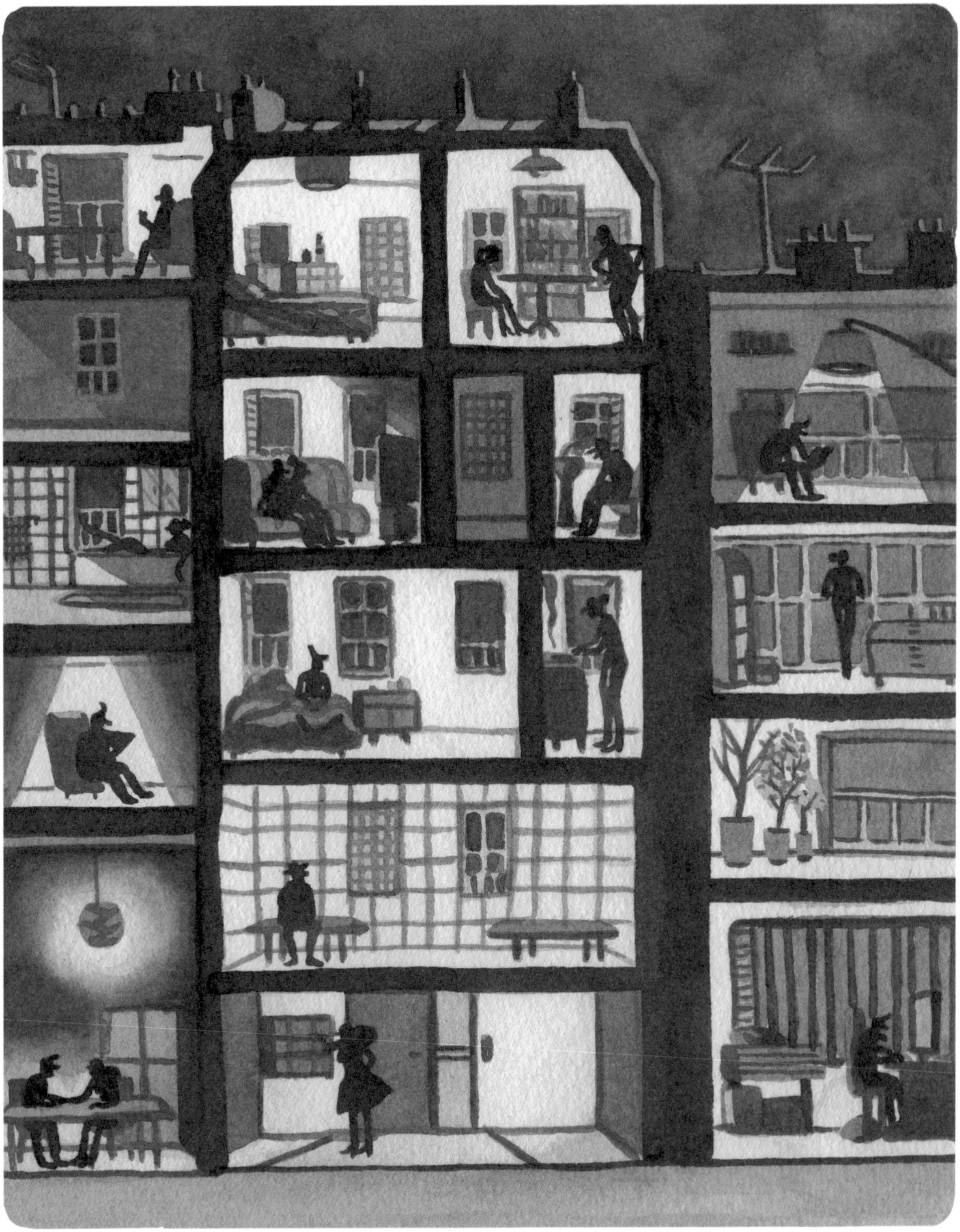

zzz

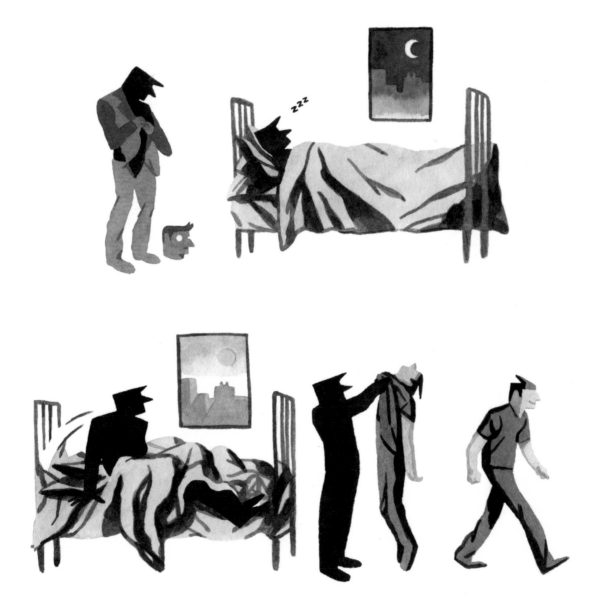

The metro: a shifting space in Paris's subterranean realm.

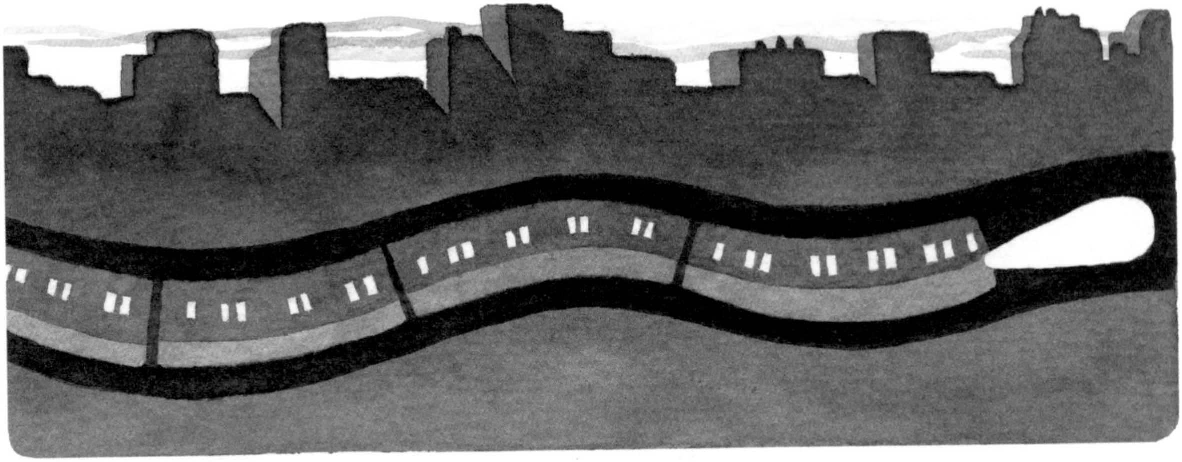

On entering, we're faced with two contradictory feelings: the unknown...

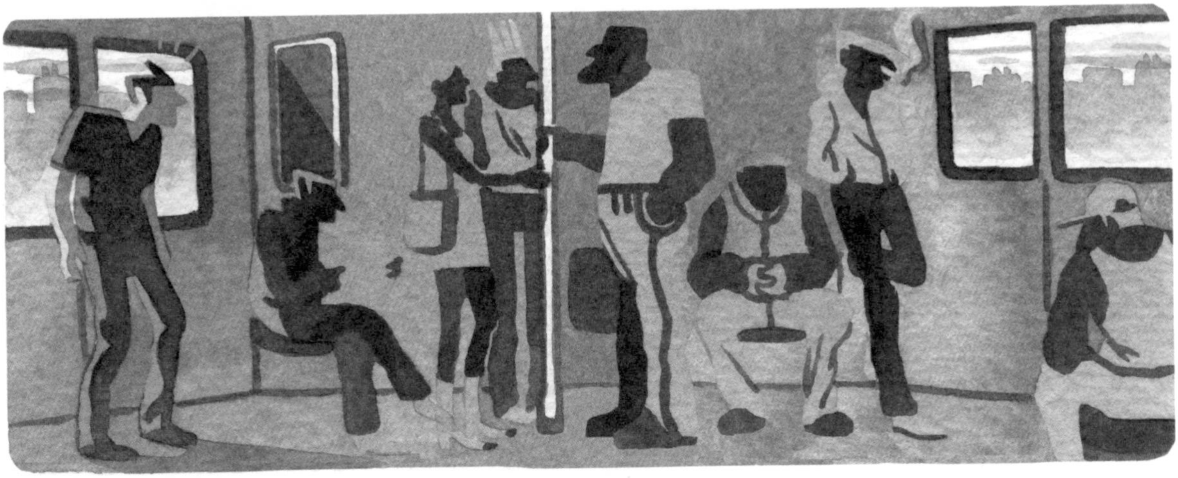

the familiar...

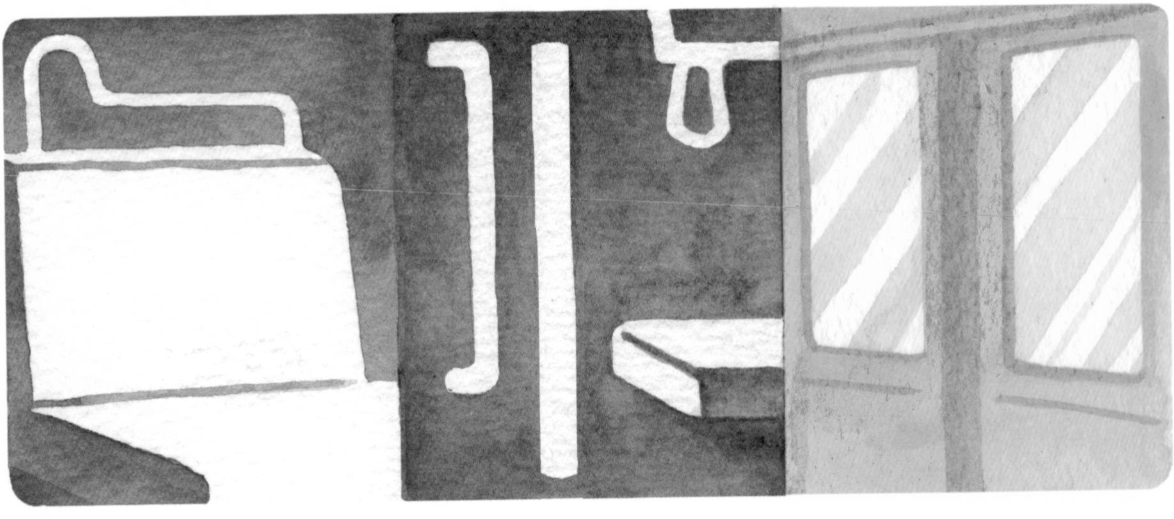

Every day, without exception, the occupants of the carriage change.

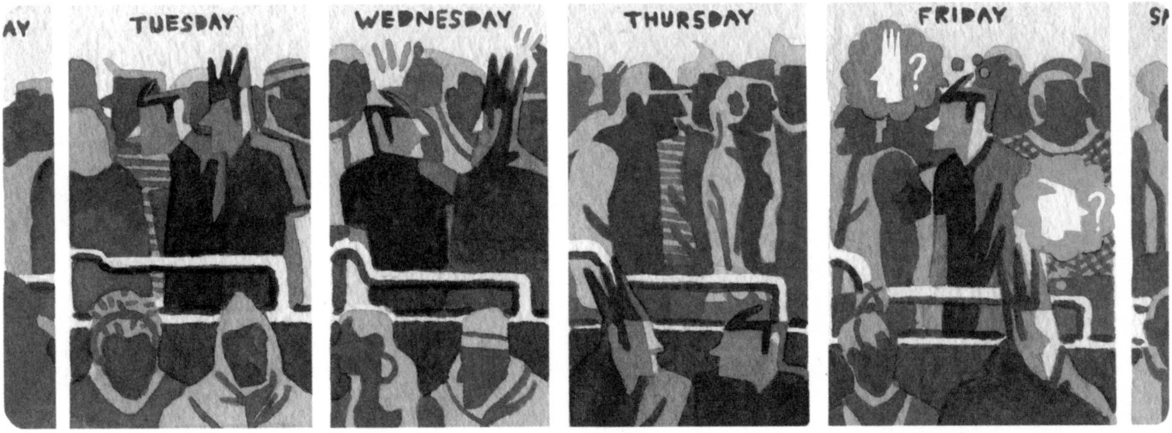
TUESDAY
WEDNESDAY
THURSDAY
FRIDAY

At each station, new passengers enter and subtly reshape our environment...

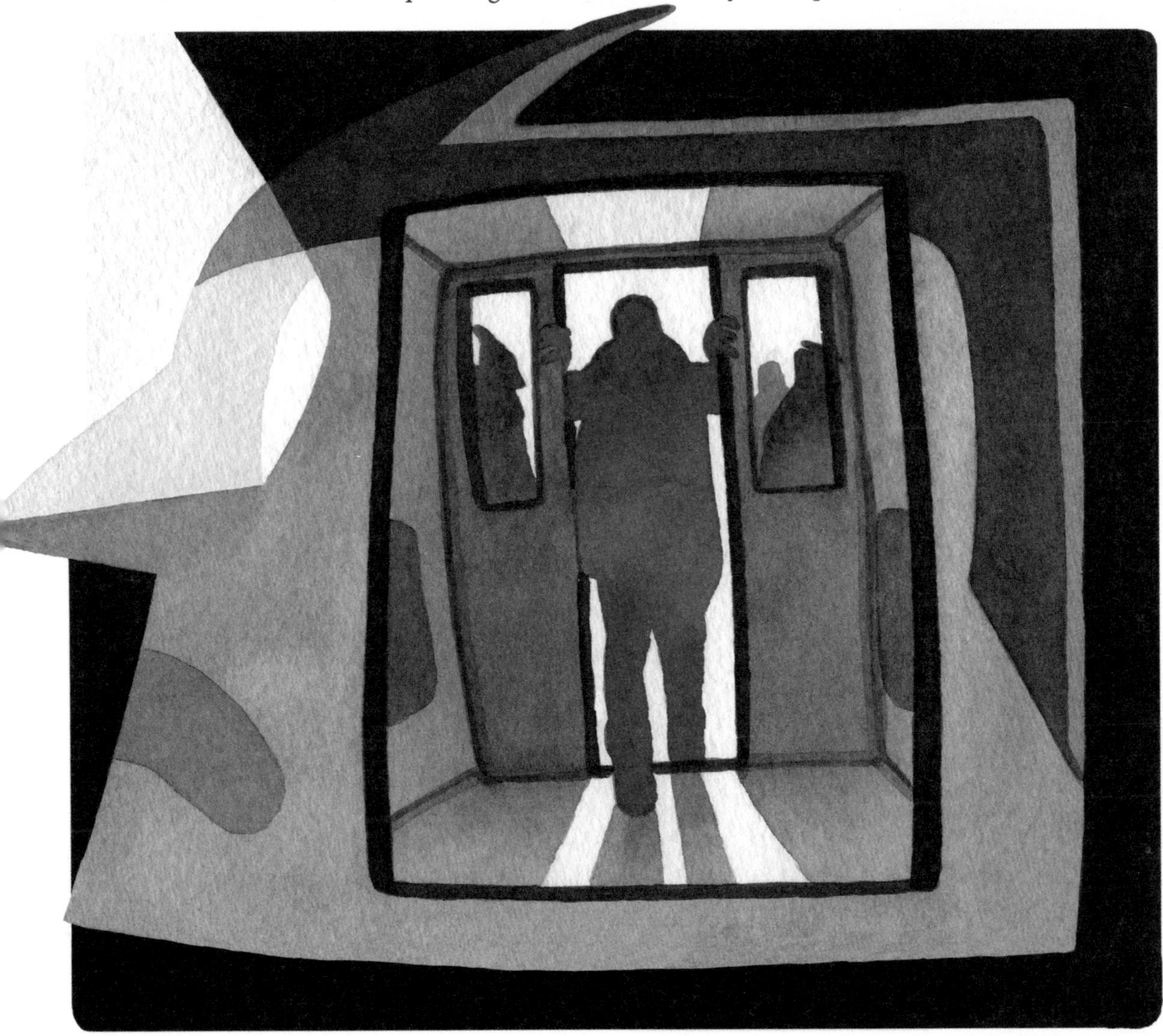

Whenever an intruder invades their territory, the other passengers turn their eyes towards him and silently validate his right of entry.

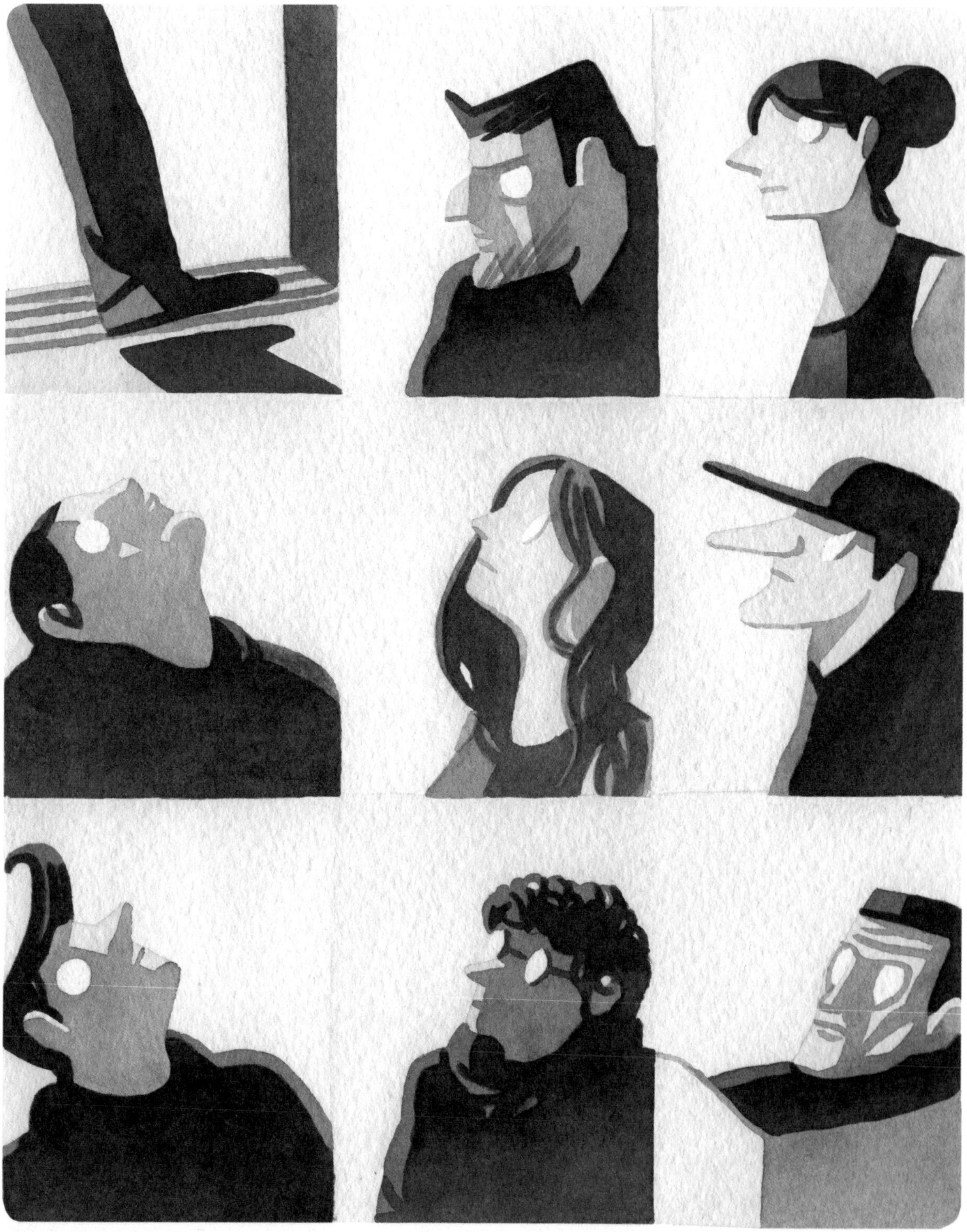

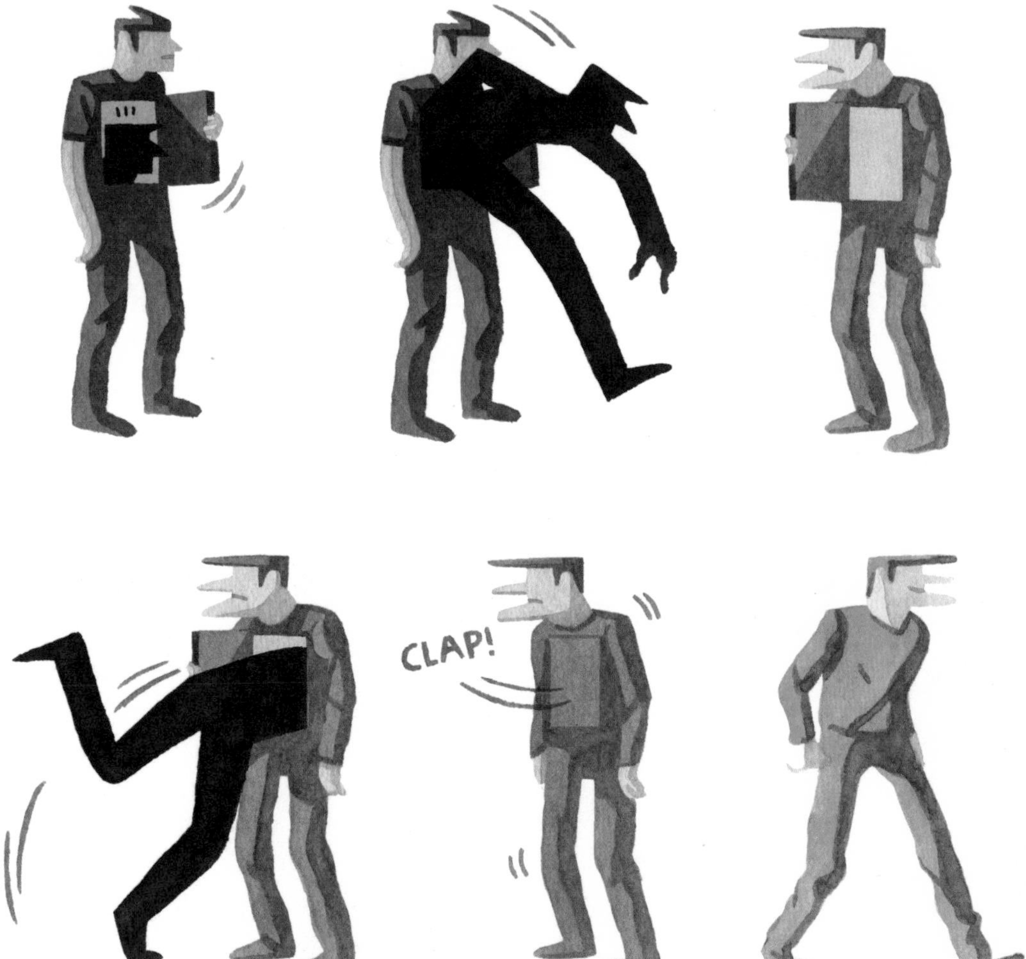
CLAP!

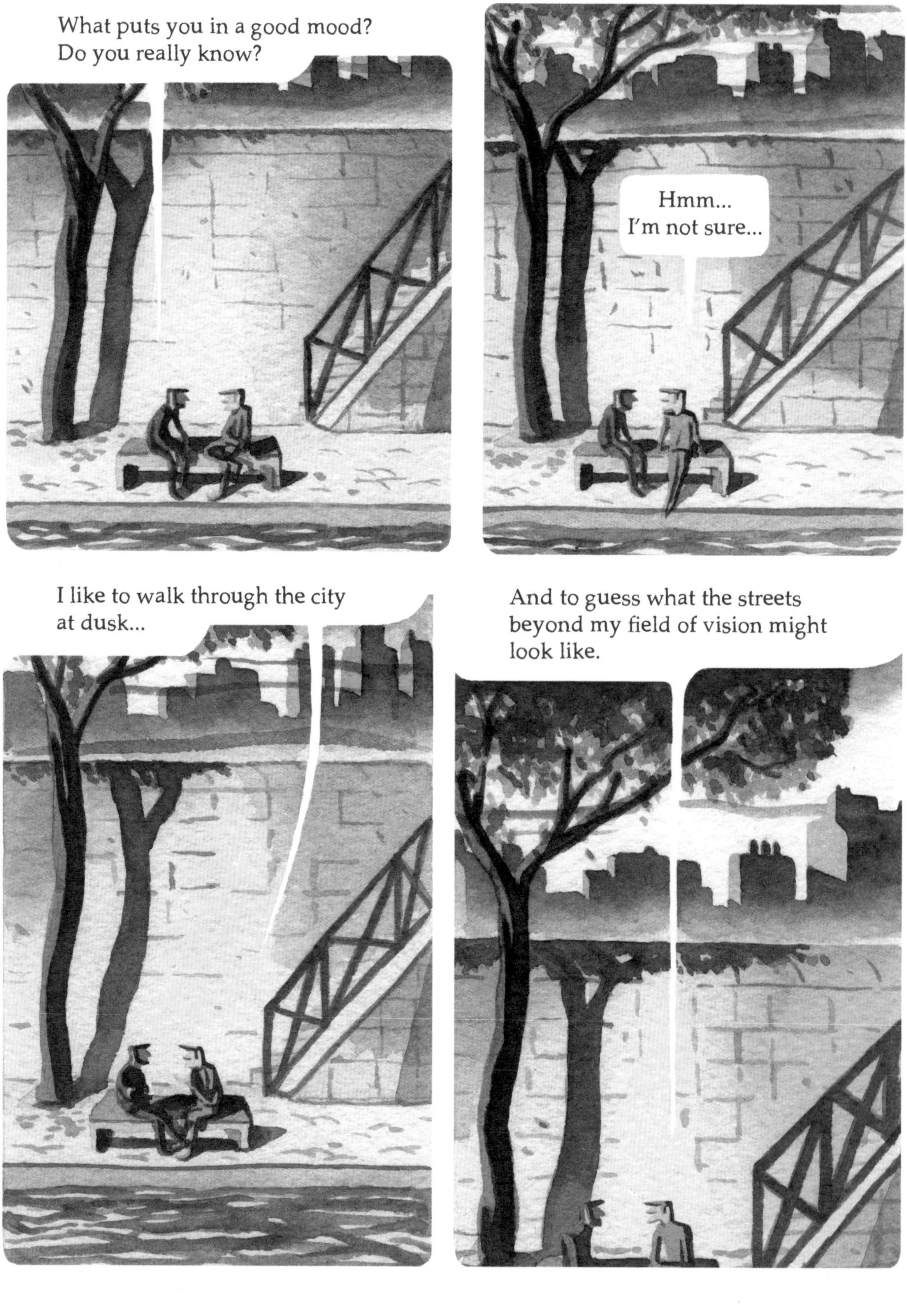
What puts you in a good mood?
Do you really know?
Hmm...
I'm not sure...
I like to walk through the city
at dusk...
And to guess what the streets
beyond my field of vision might
look like.

The ones hidden behind a row of buildings, waiting only to be discovered.

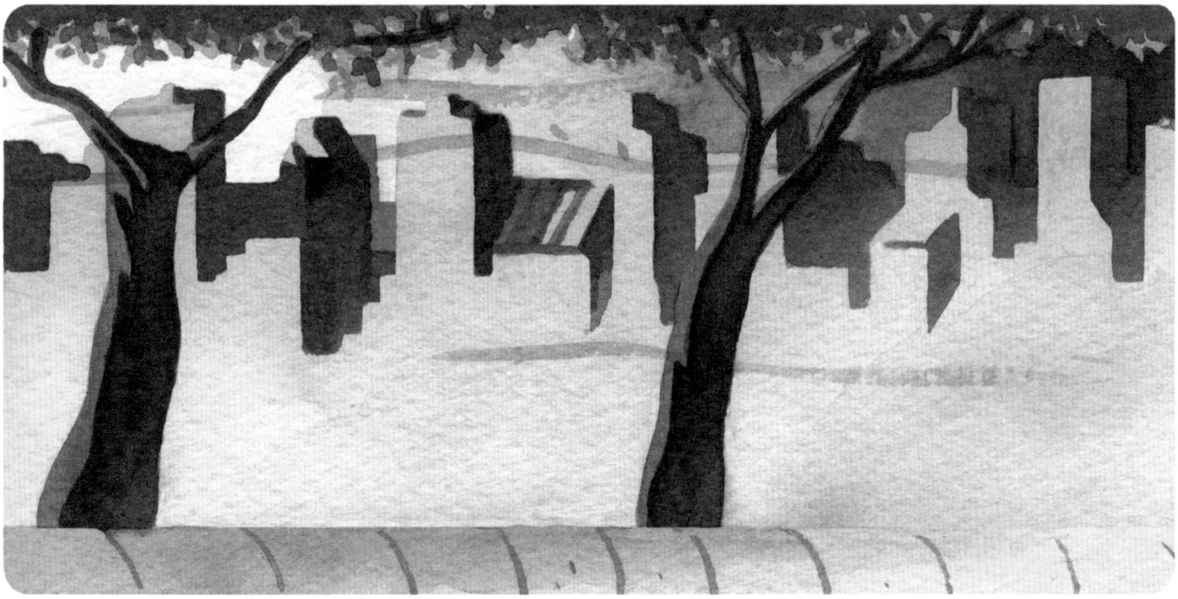

I dream of walking through walls... creating my own route.

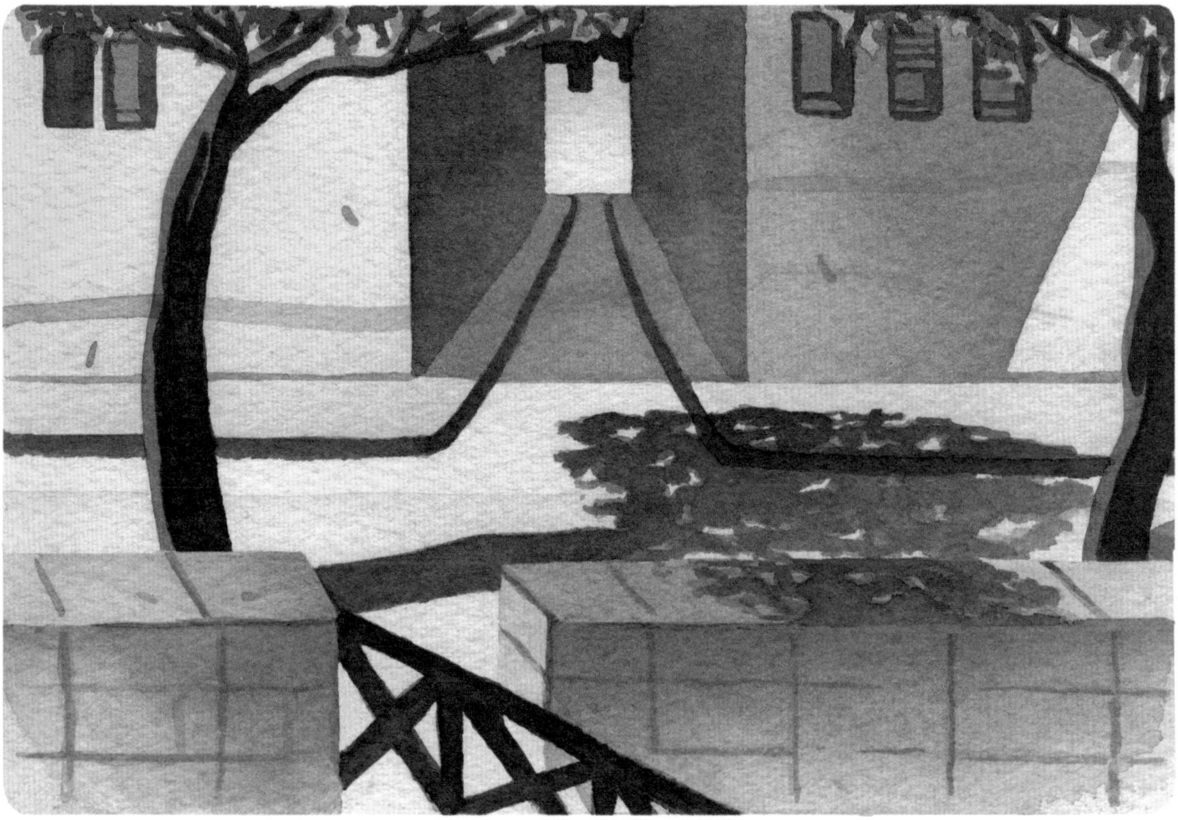

There's always a crucial moment in these wanderings...

I approach the end of a street. I become impatient, curious as to what I might find.

  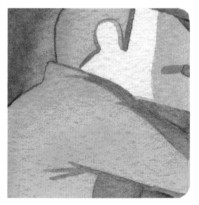

A beguiling back street, full of charm?

A wide avenue, cold and austere?

A banal street, like so many others?

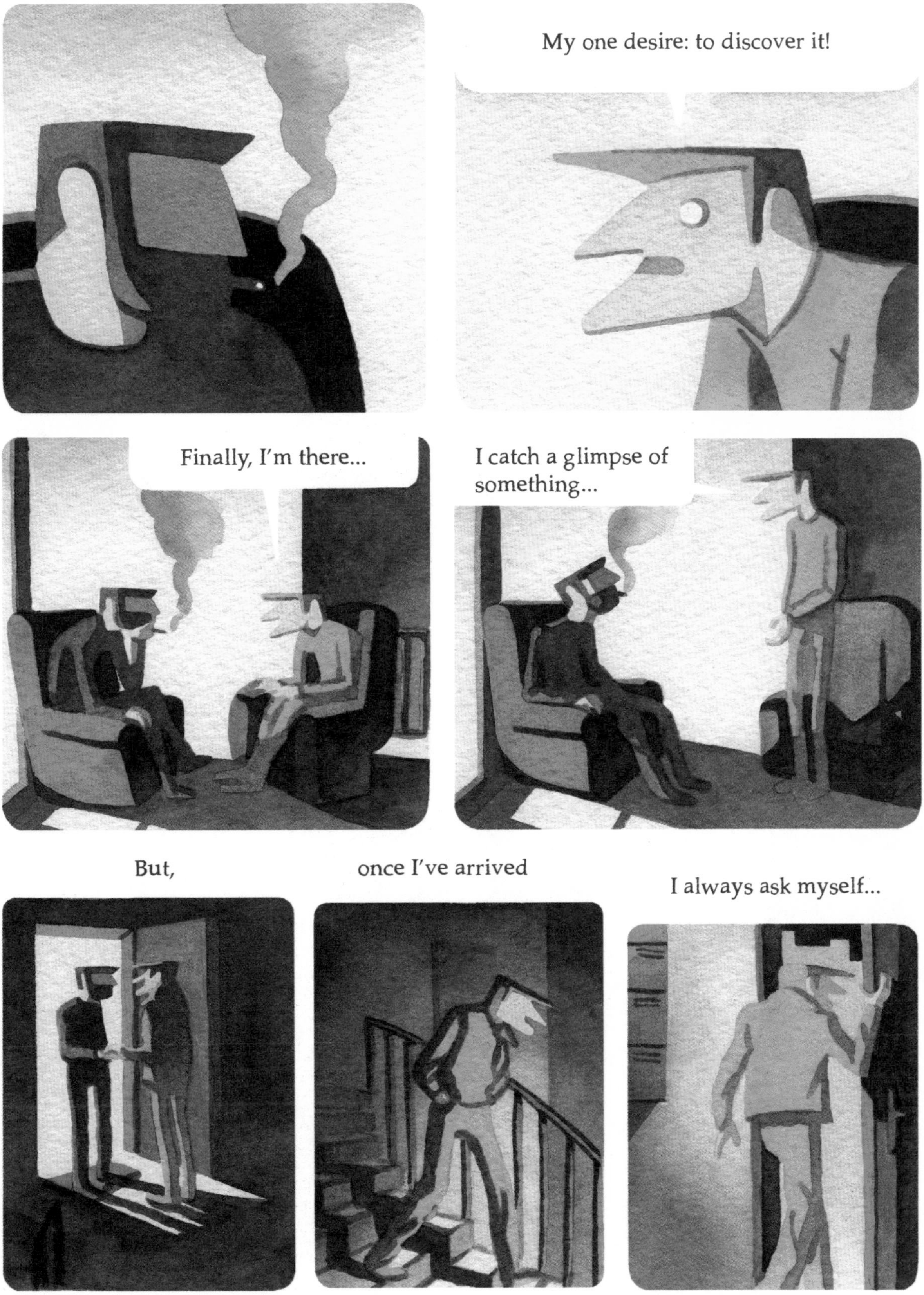
My one desire: to discover it!
Finally, I'm there...
I catch a glimpse of something...
But,
once I've arrived
I always ask myself...

"Does the place I'm searching for in this maze of a city really exist?"

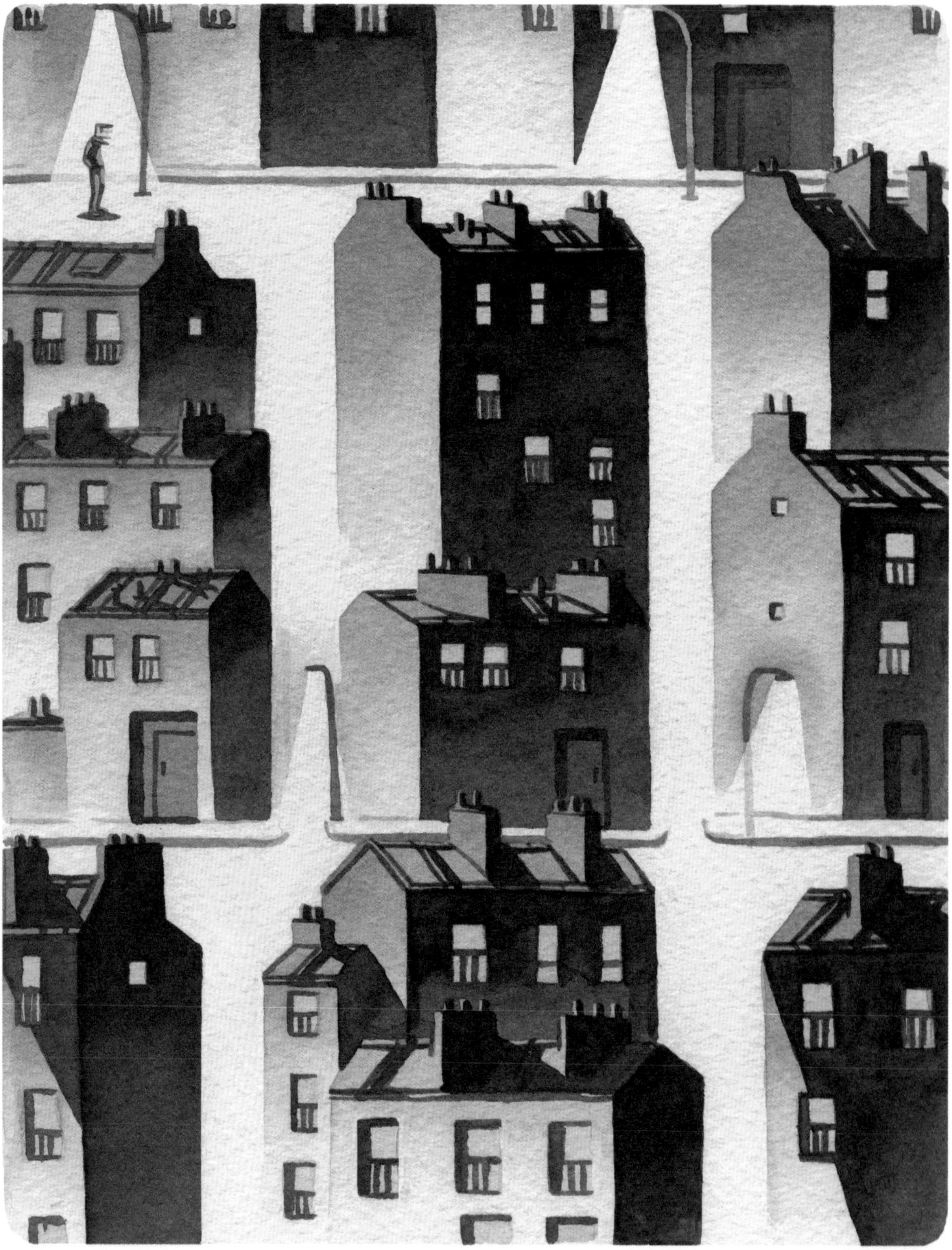

CLING
CLING
CLING

PAF!

CLING
CLING
CLING

PAF!

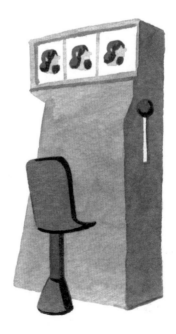

This morning I buy some bread. Taking my change, I recognise one of the coins!

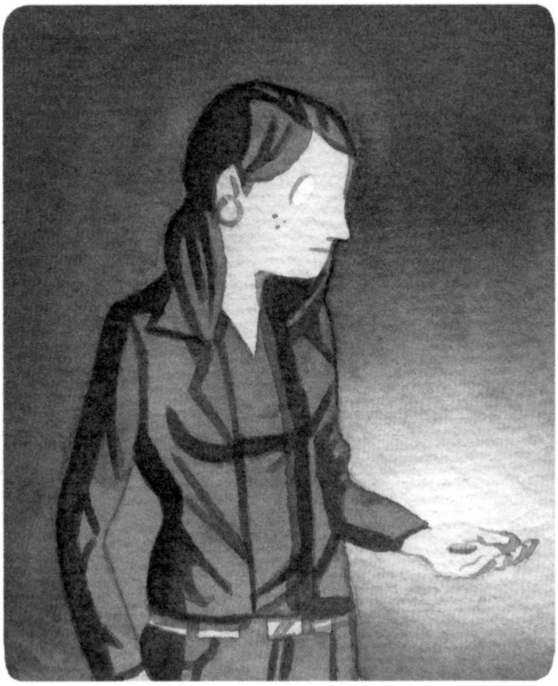

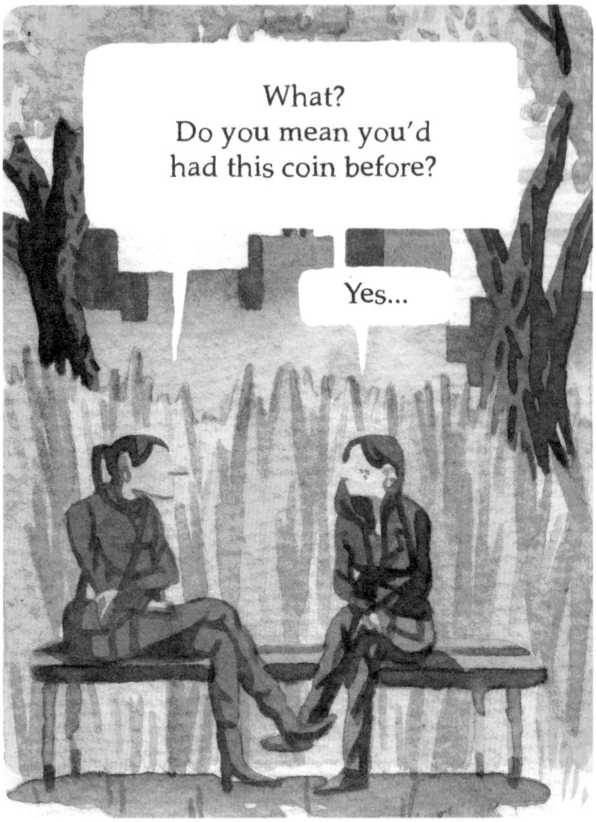
What? Do you mean you'd had this coin before?
Yes...

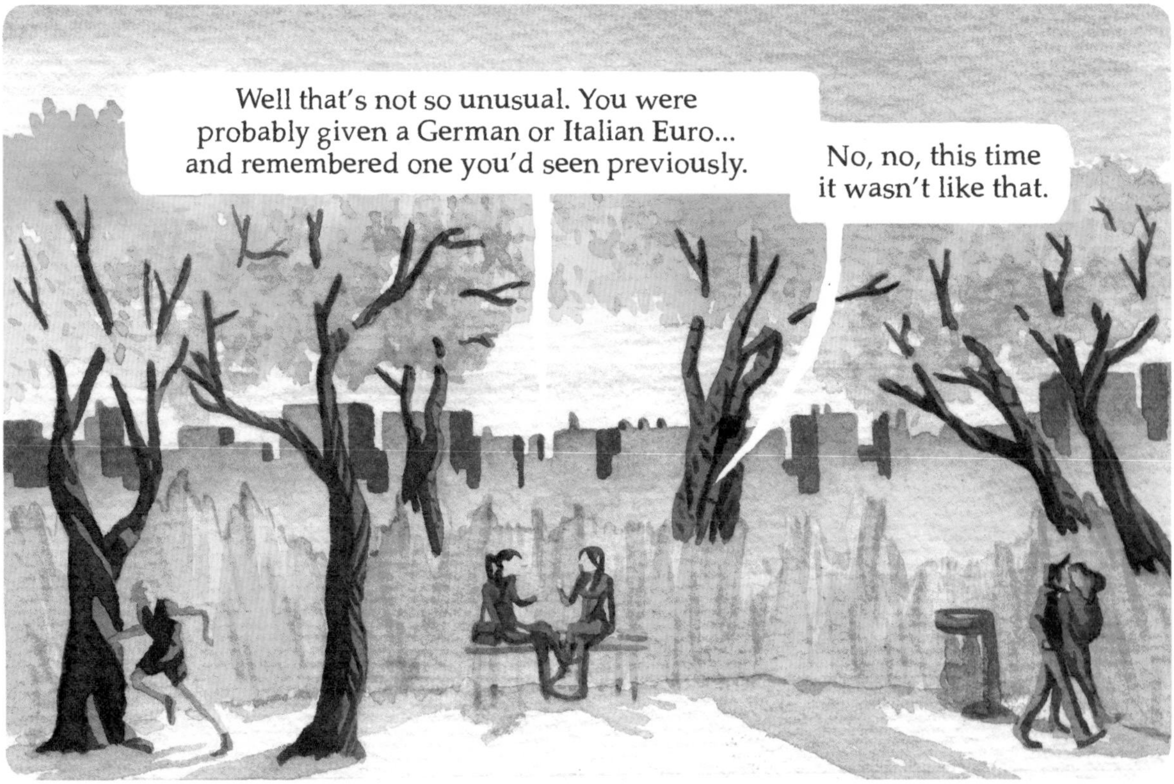
Well that's not so unusual. You were probably given a German or Italian Euro... and remembered one you'd seen previously.
No, no, this time it wasn't like that.

This particular coin – I'd held it in my hand before, I'm sure of it.

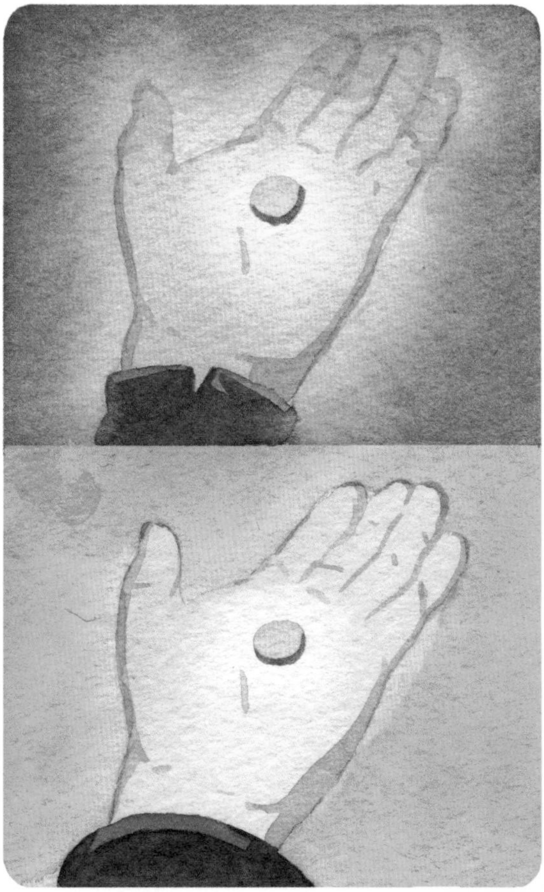

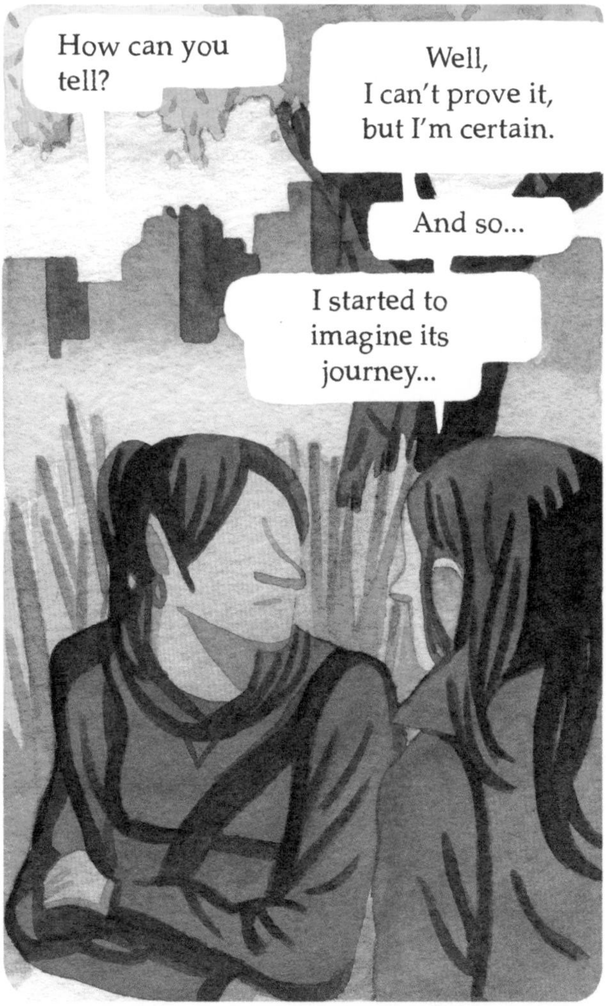
How can you tell?
Well, I can't prove it, but I'm certain.
And so...
I started to imagine its journey...

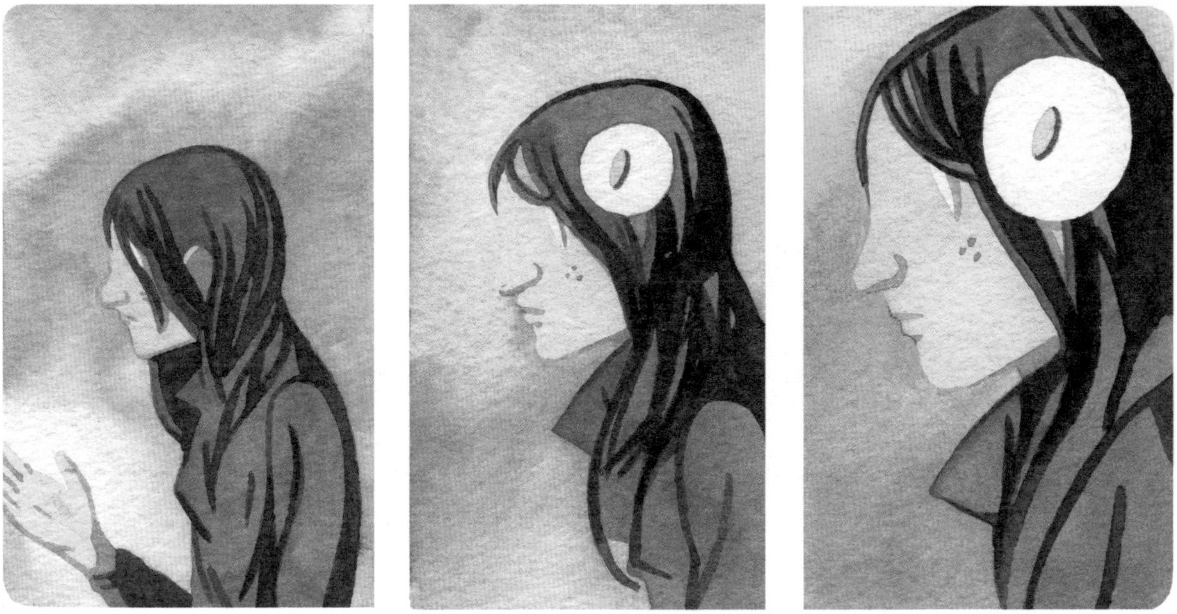

Maybe it had once belonged to a rich businessman?

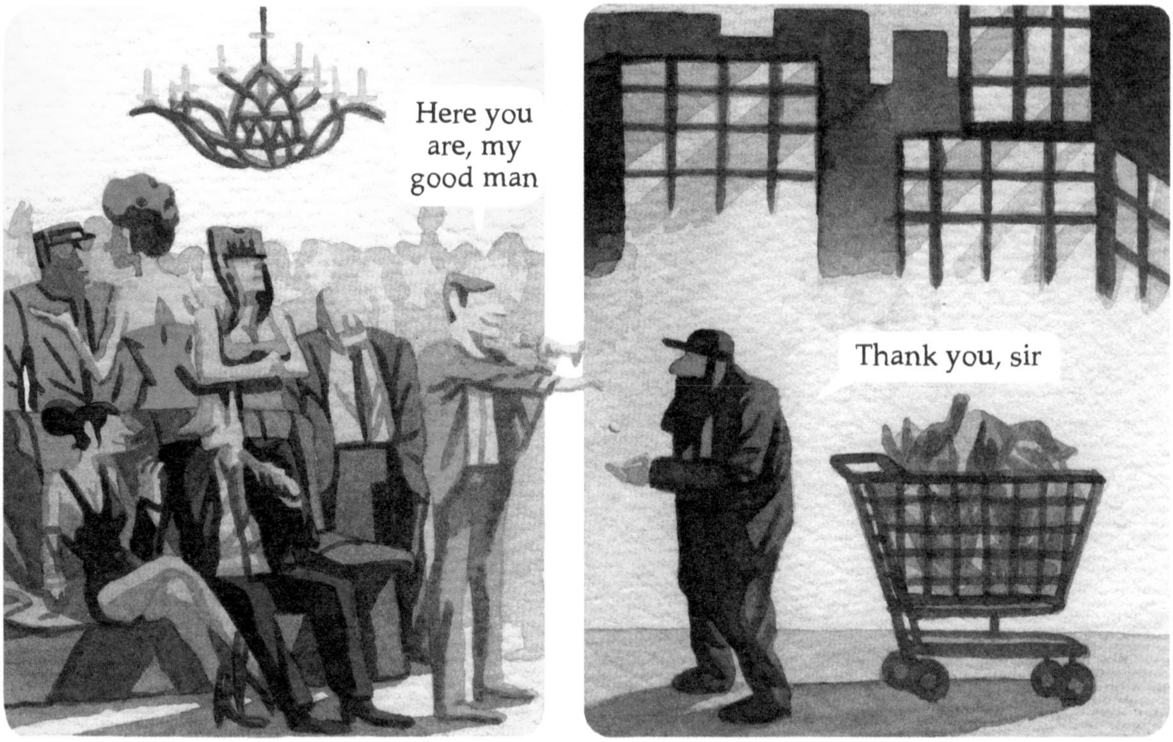
Here you are, my good man
Thank you, sir

Then it ended up in an international star's handbag!

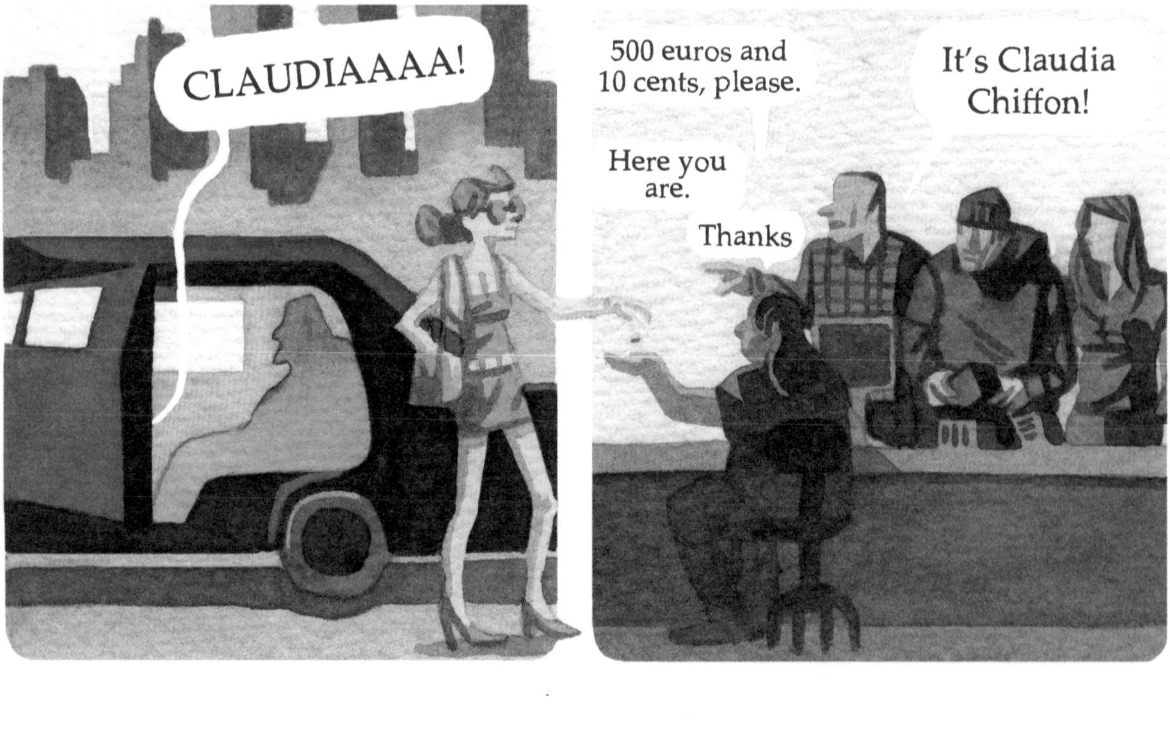
CLAUDIAAAA!
500 euros and 10 cents, please.
Here you are.
Thanks
It's Claudia Chiffon!

This coin must have seen quite a bit of the world as it passed from the hands of one traveller to another. Obviously, I didn't know where it had been... but imagining its journey... entertained me!

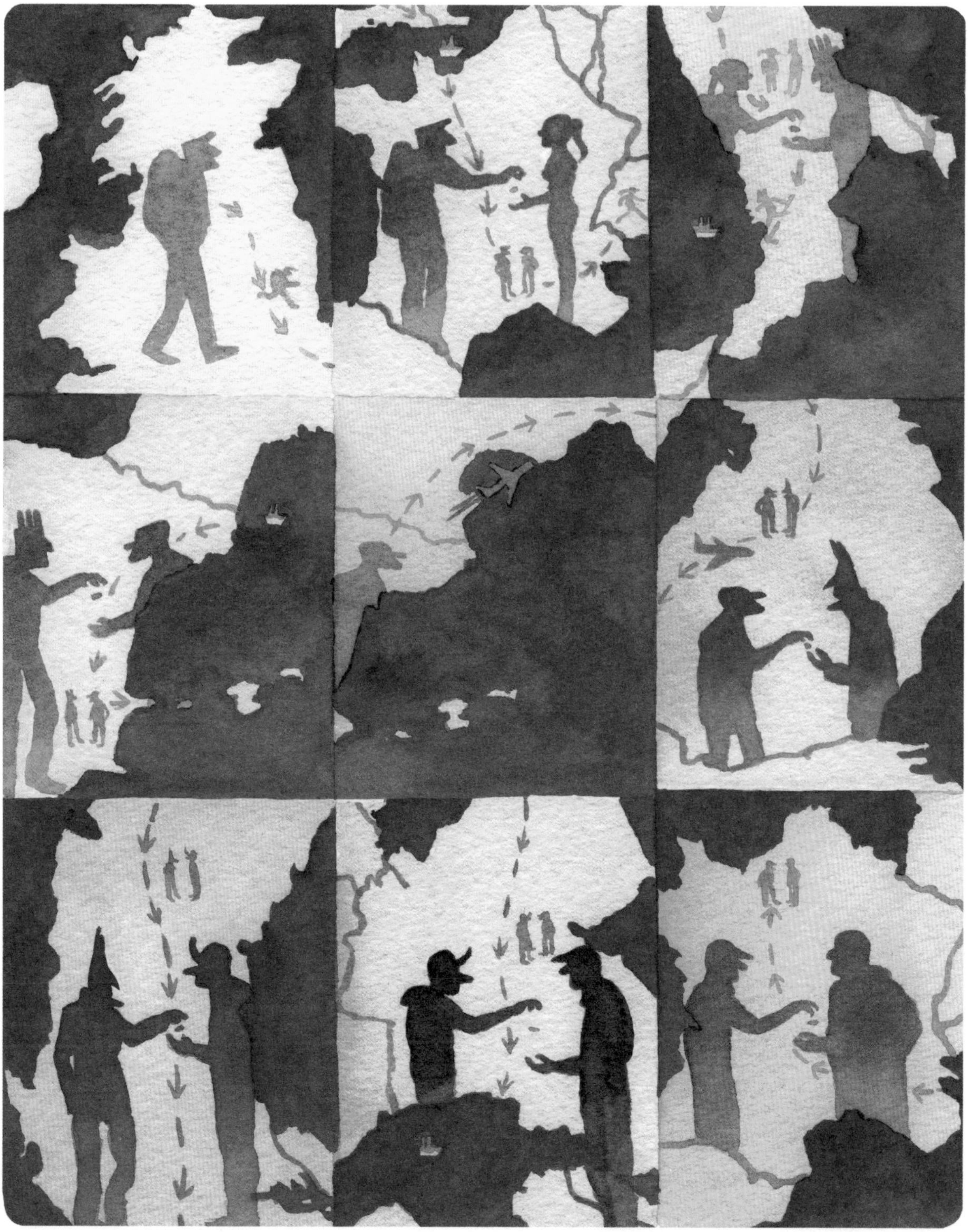

In vain, I tried to make sense of its reappearance...

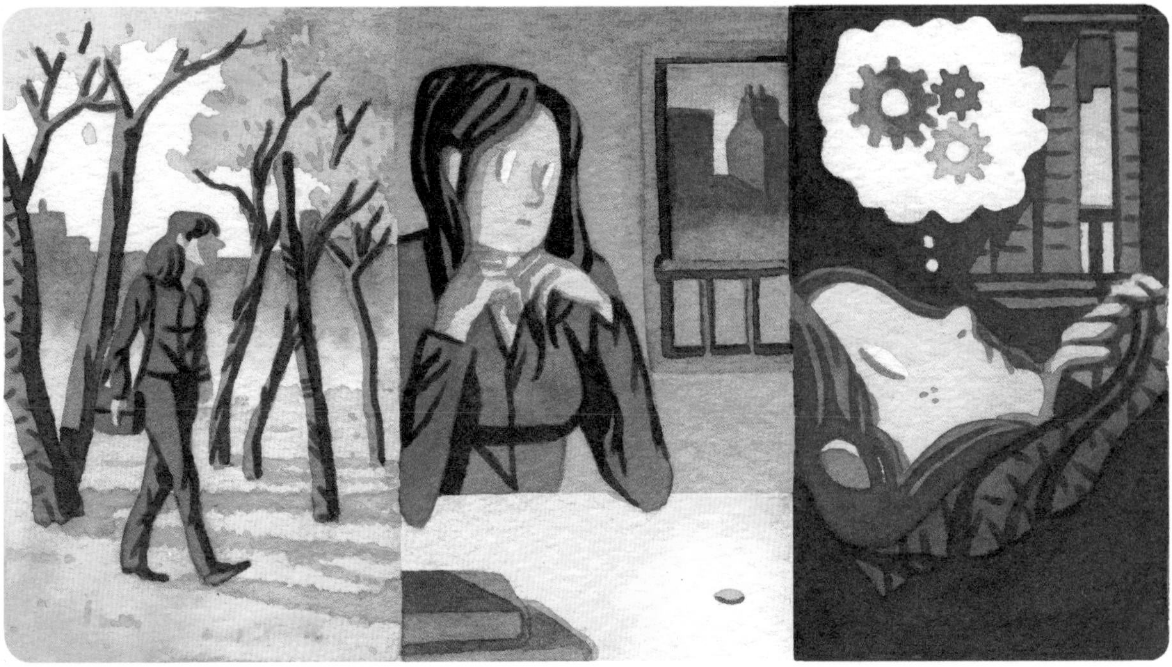

With no rational explanation, I decided to let it go, and slipped the coin into my purse.

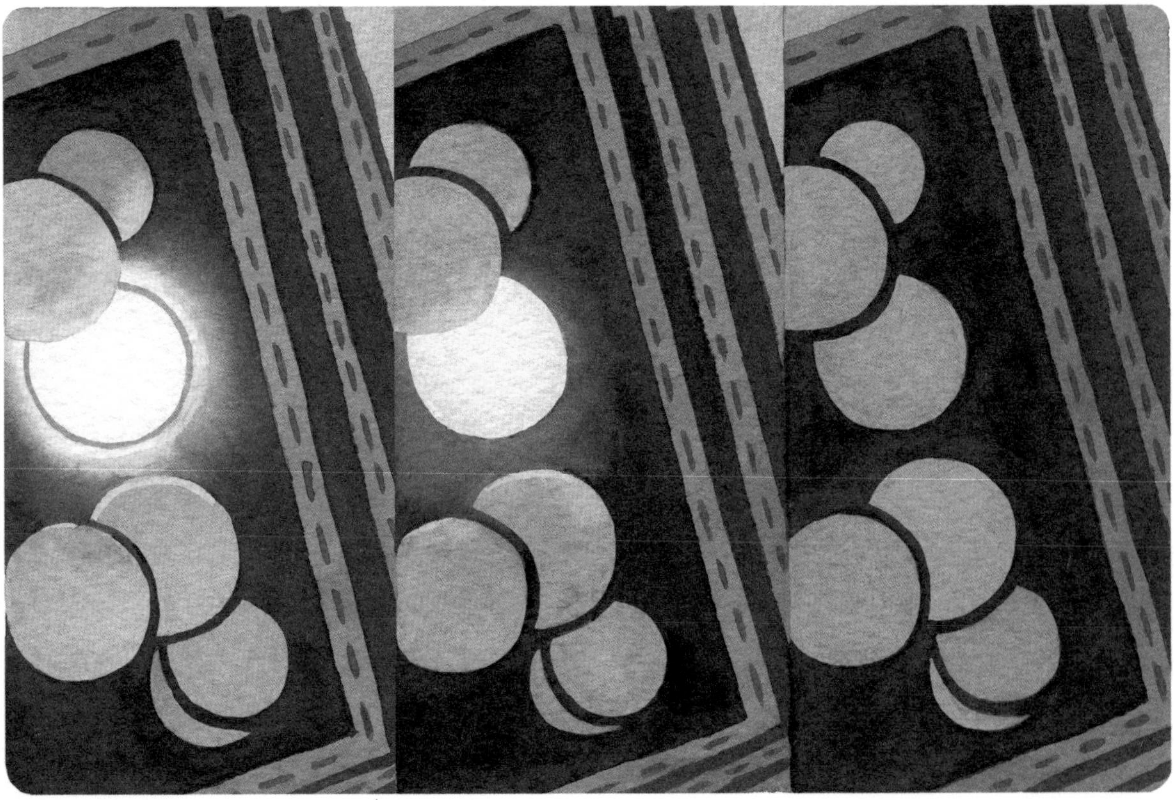

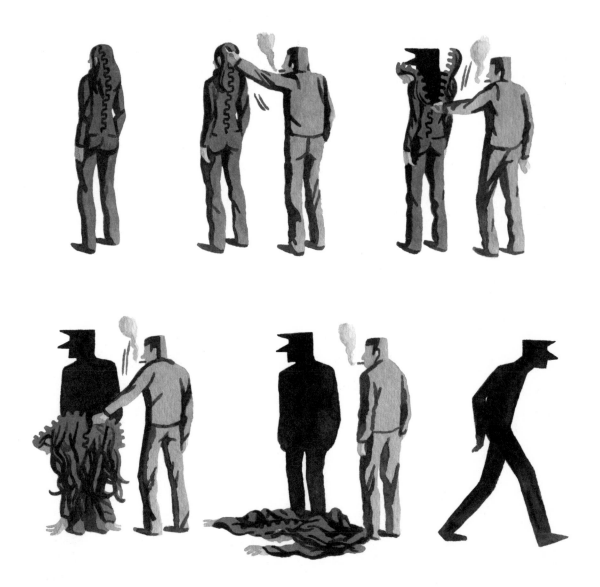

The metro flies above Paris, sailing against the wind to its own rattling rhythm.

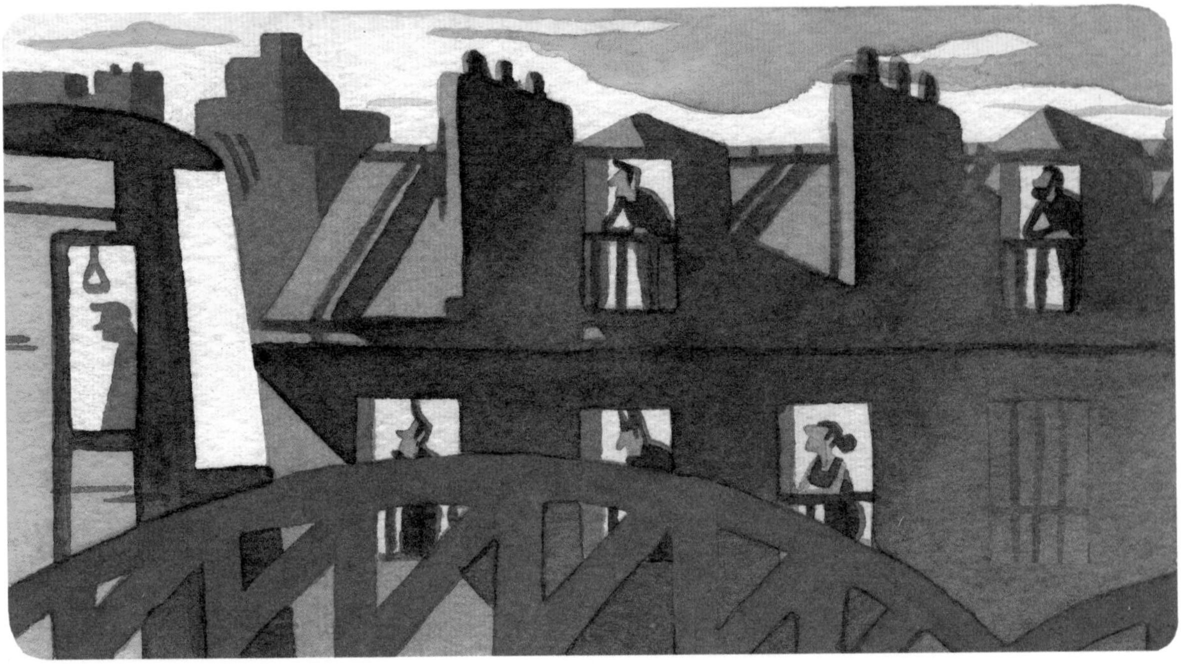

It is the Parisians' ephemeral and shifting home.

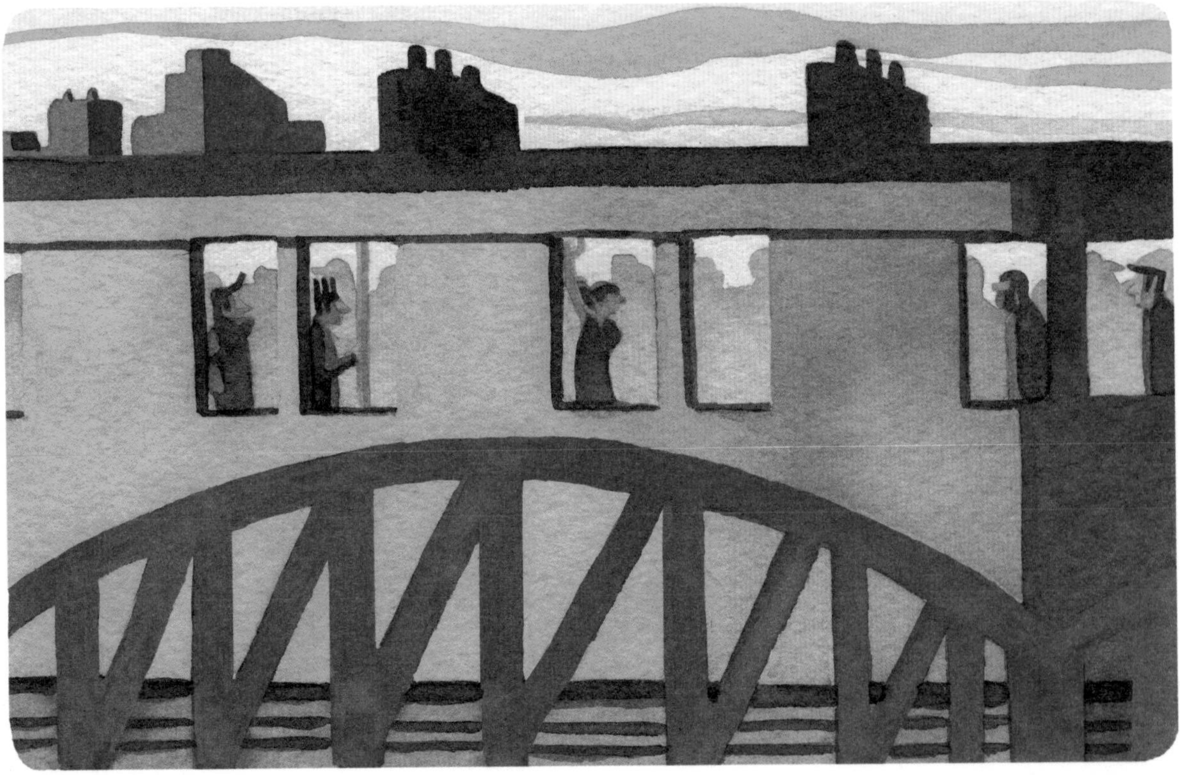

Above their heads, it travels through the ages...

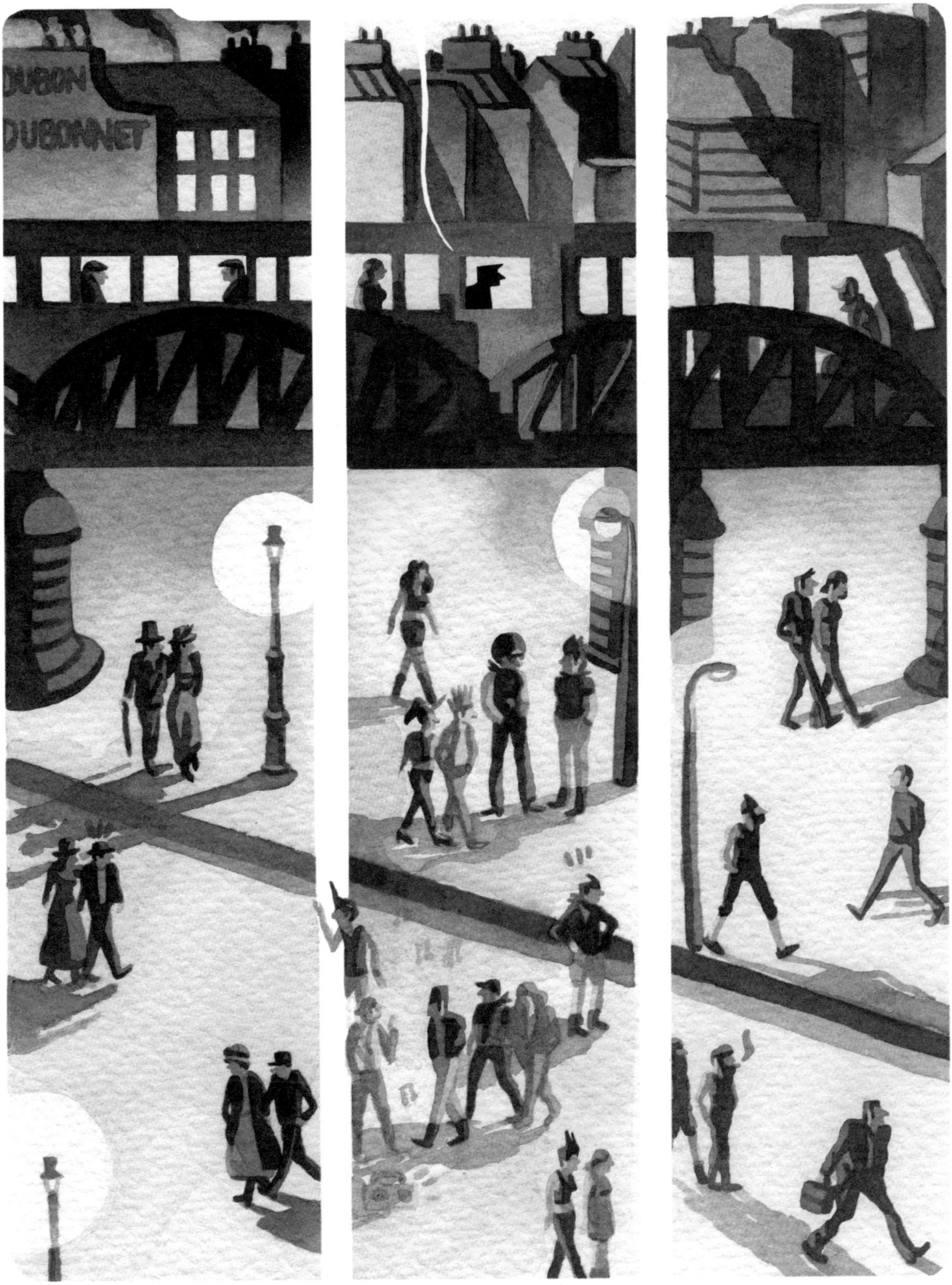
DUBON
DUBONNET

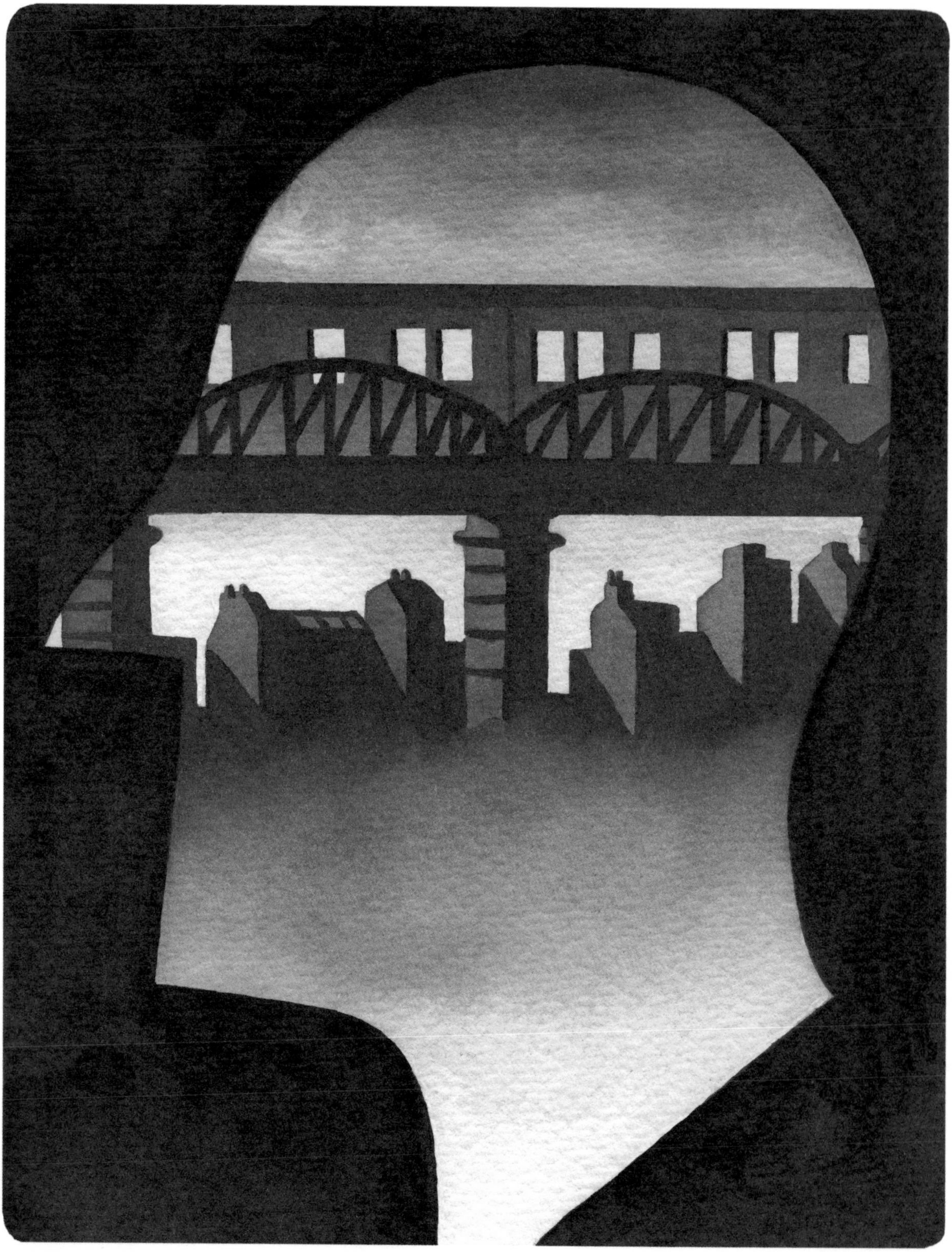

And its radiant imprint is indelible...

CLAP!

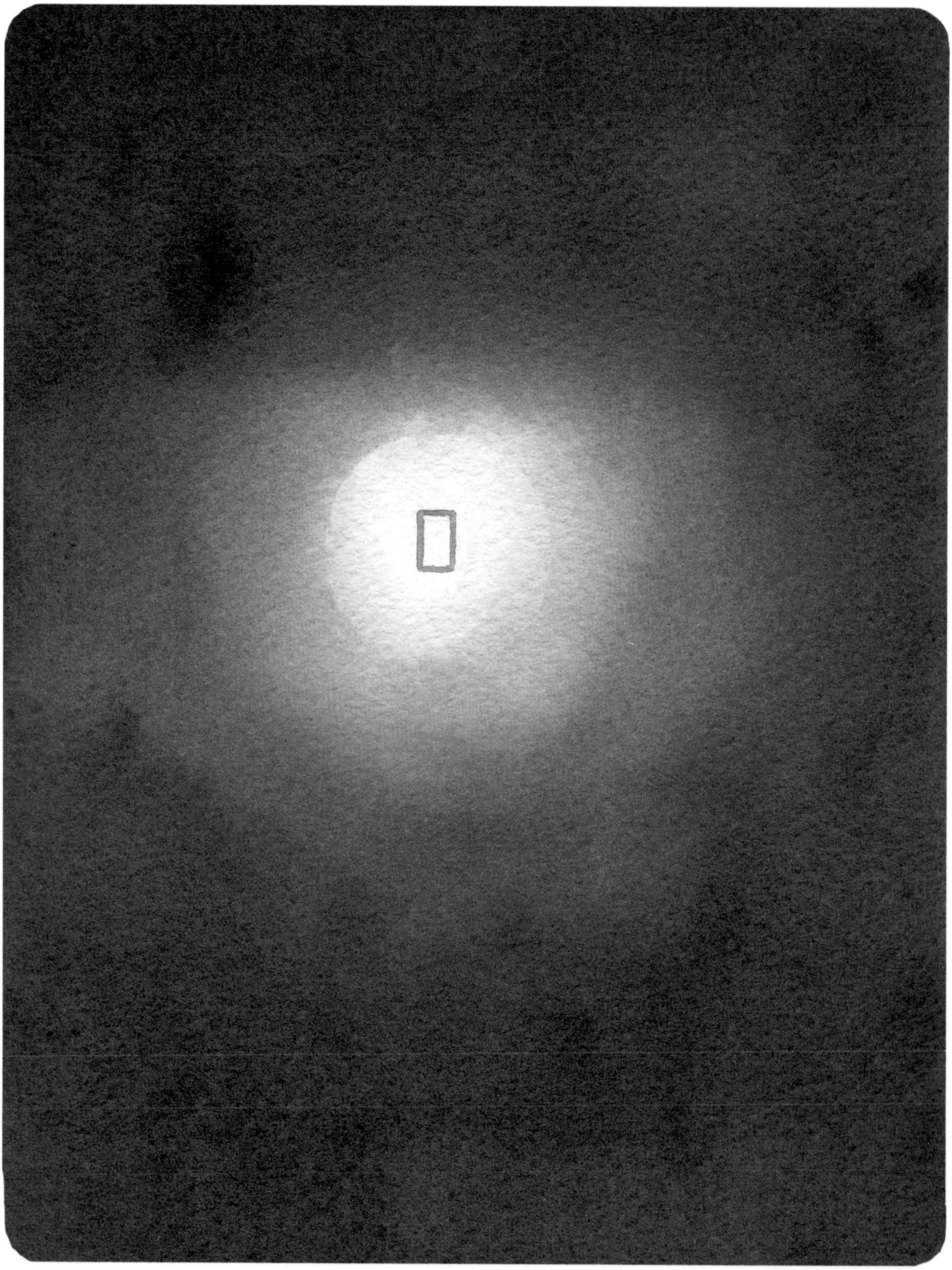

In the distance I glimpse a window, like a mirage in the desert....

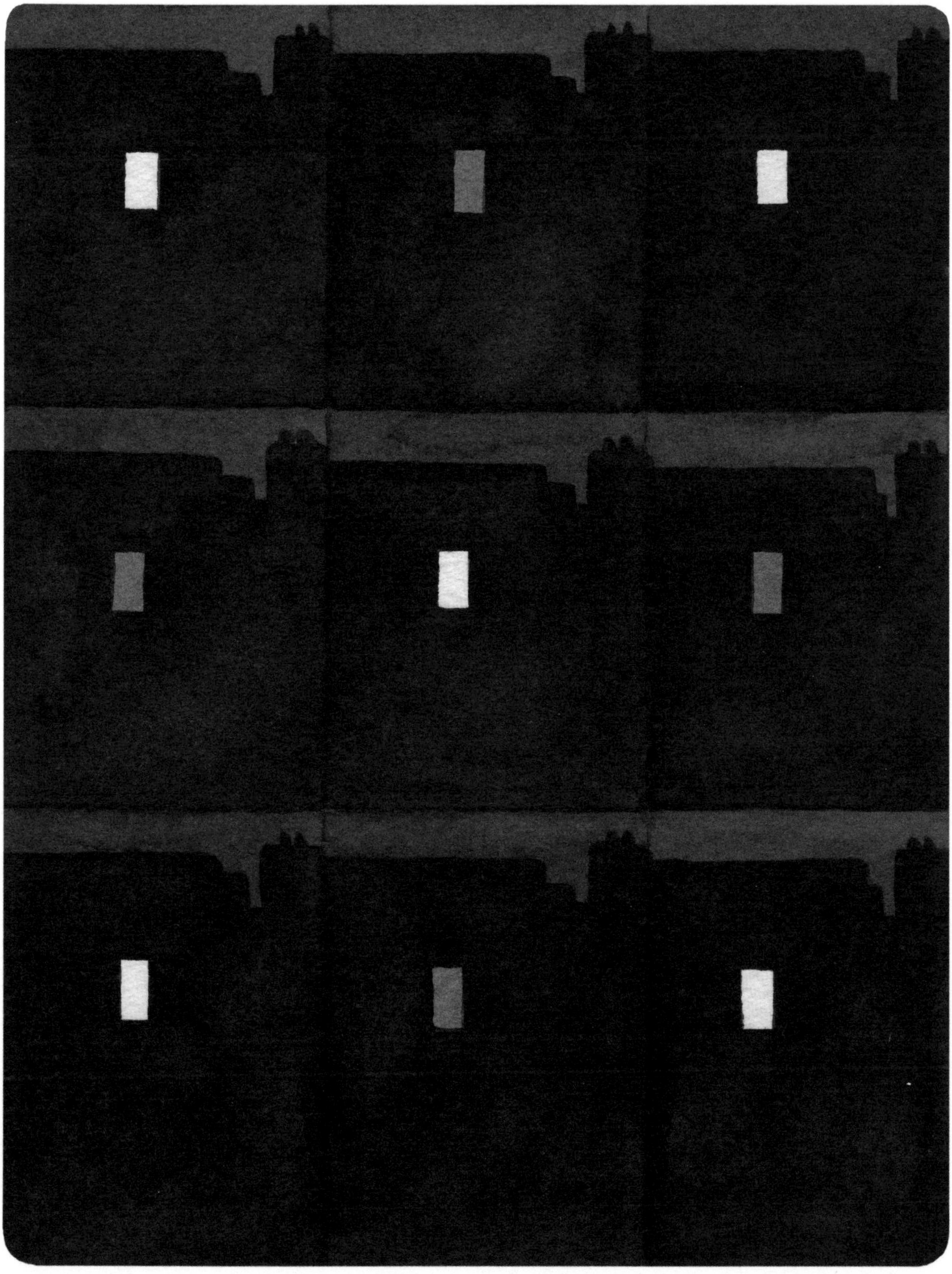

It pulses in the night...

Ever dependable, its presence reassures me.

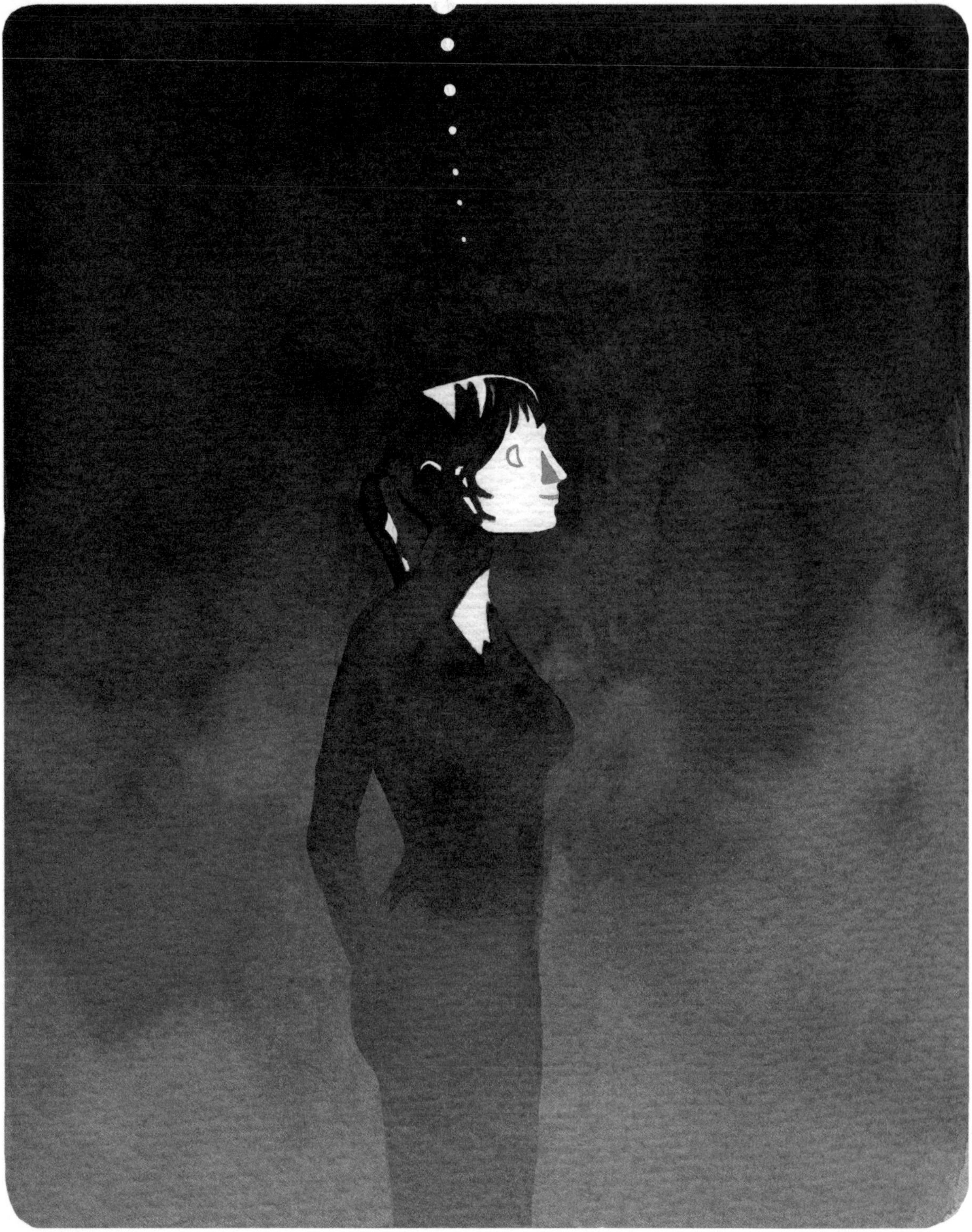

Some people, on the other hand, are obsessed; they never sleep...

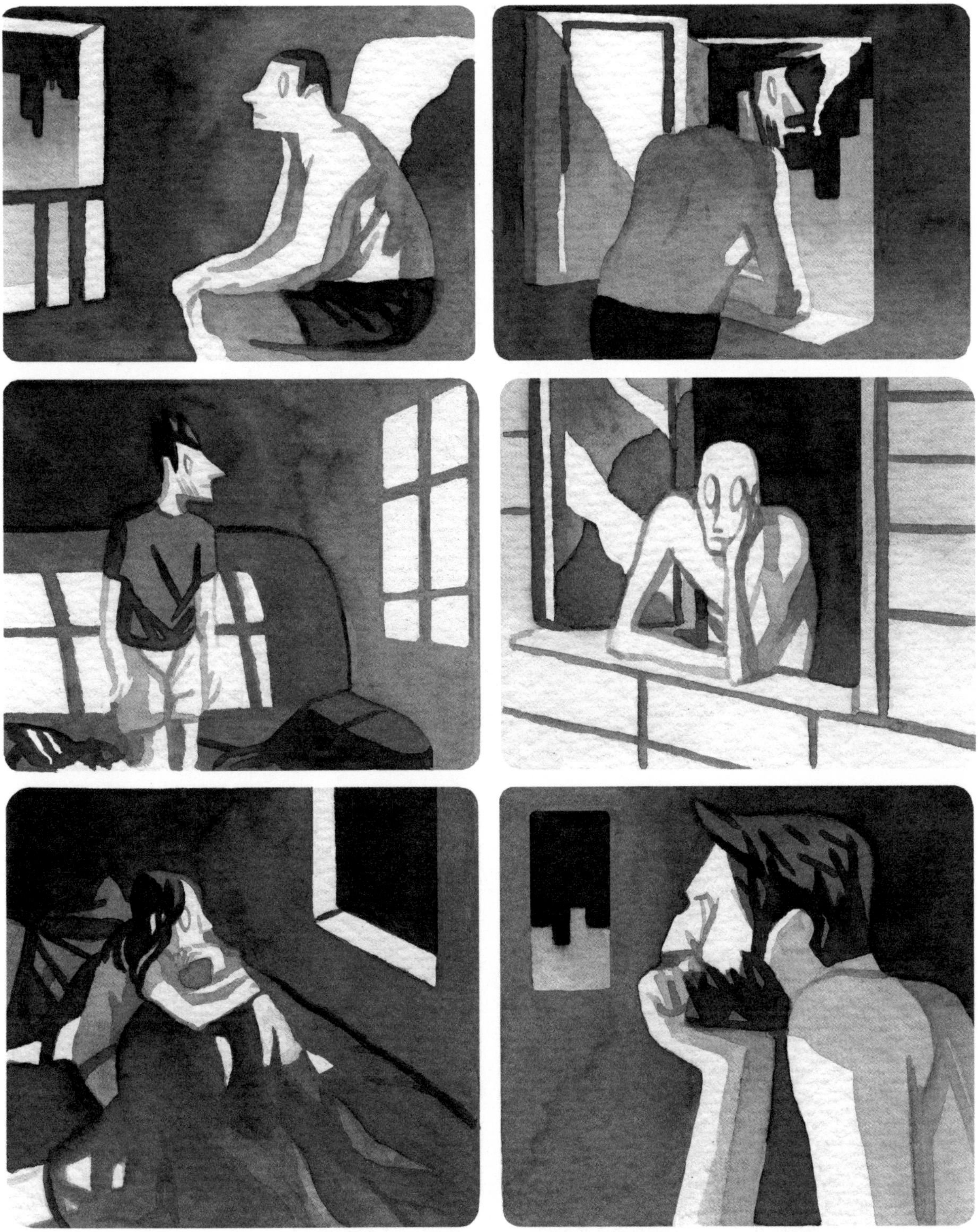

Sometimes, they happen to look away...

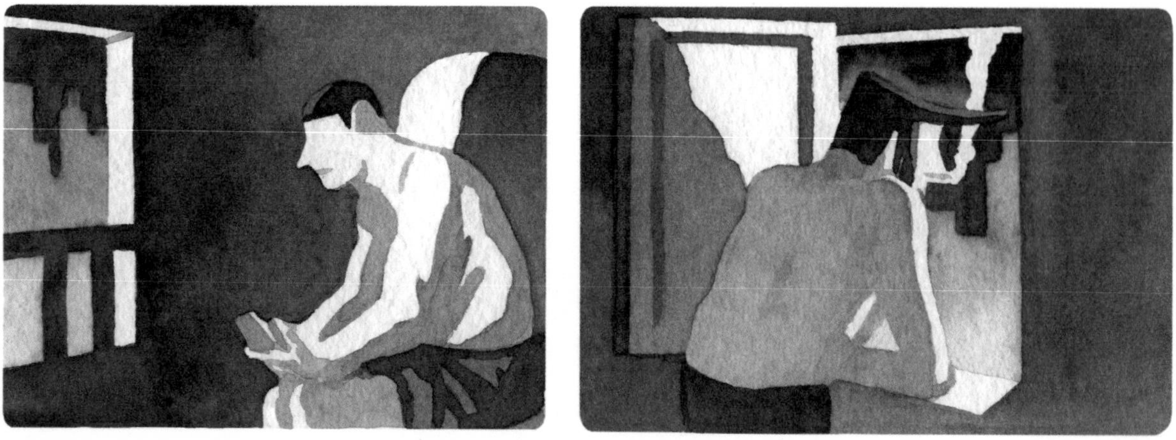

Offended, the window vanishes.

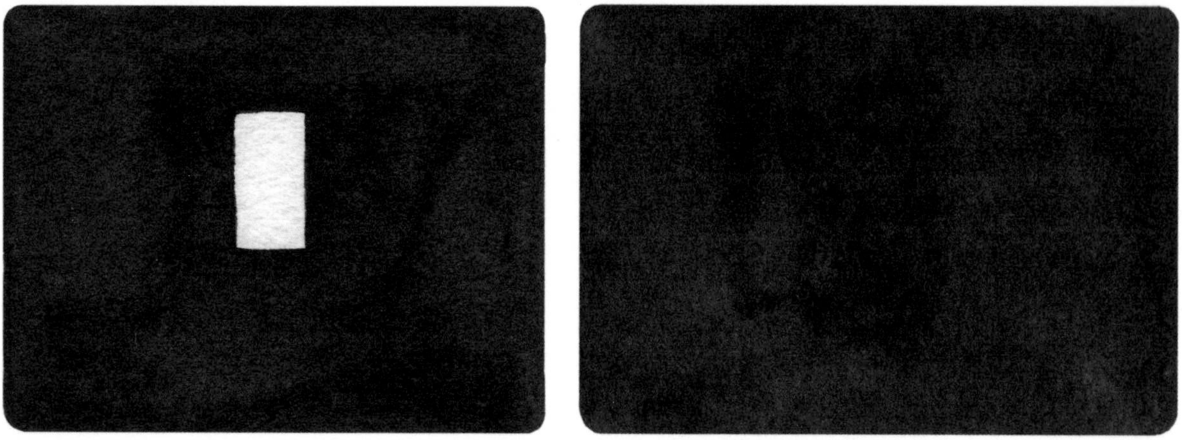

And then, disappointed, they fall asleep...

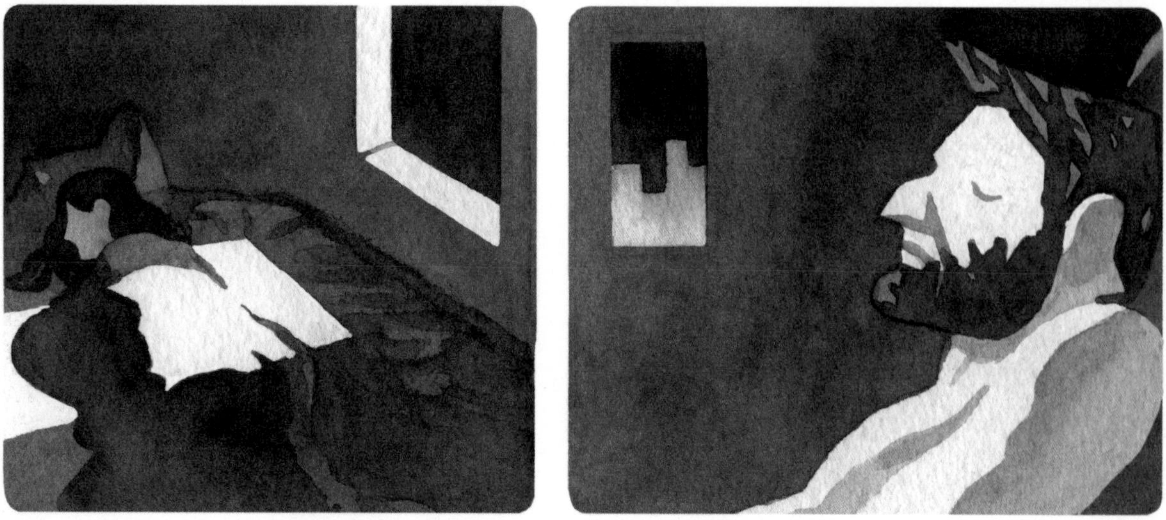

Some nights, the window reappears.

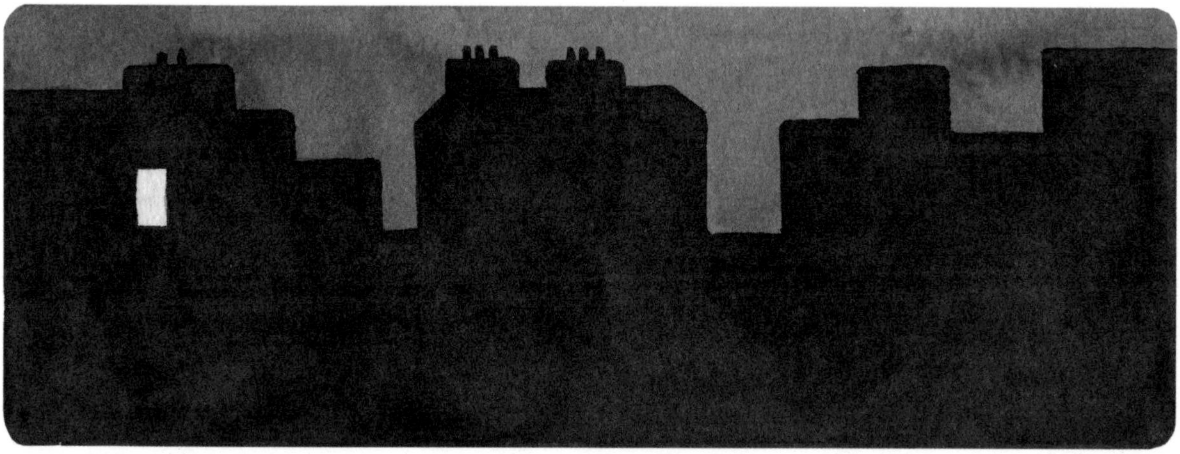

On others...

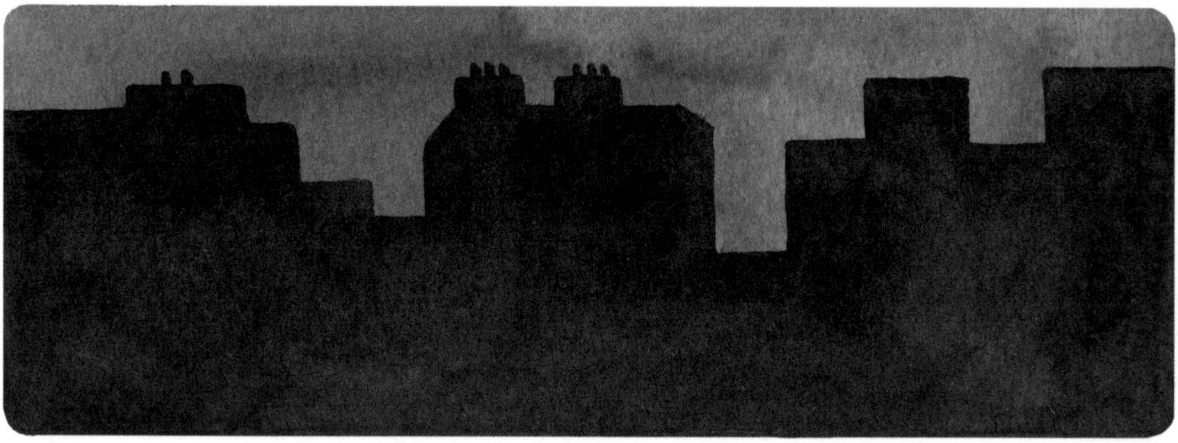

In its absence, a colleague steps in to replace it.

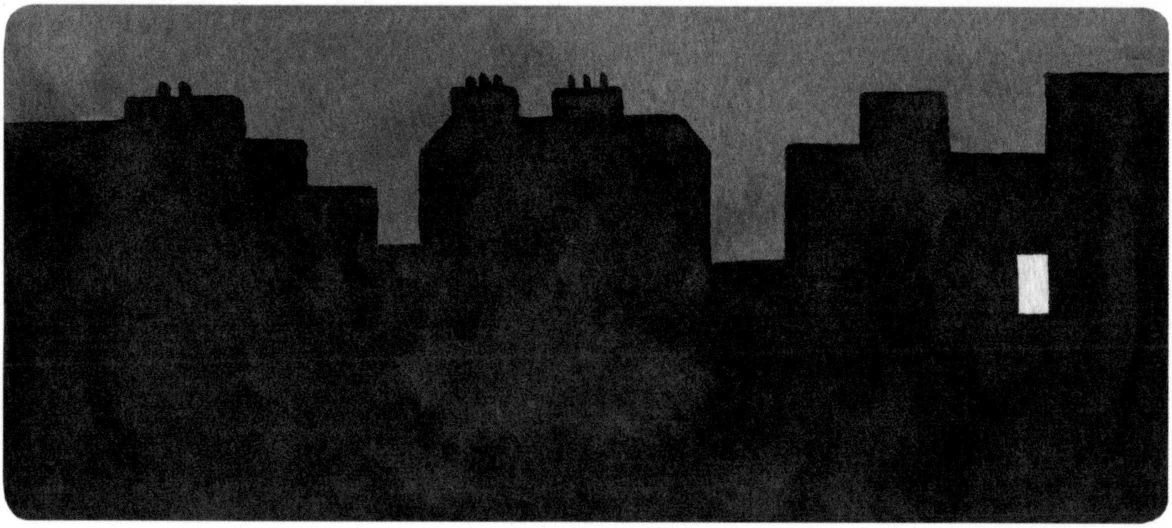

Each night offers a little tableau in which the windows light up and switch off... it's different every time.

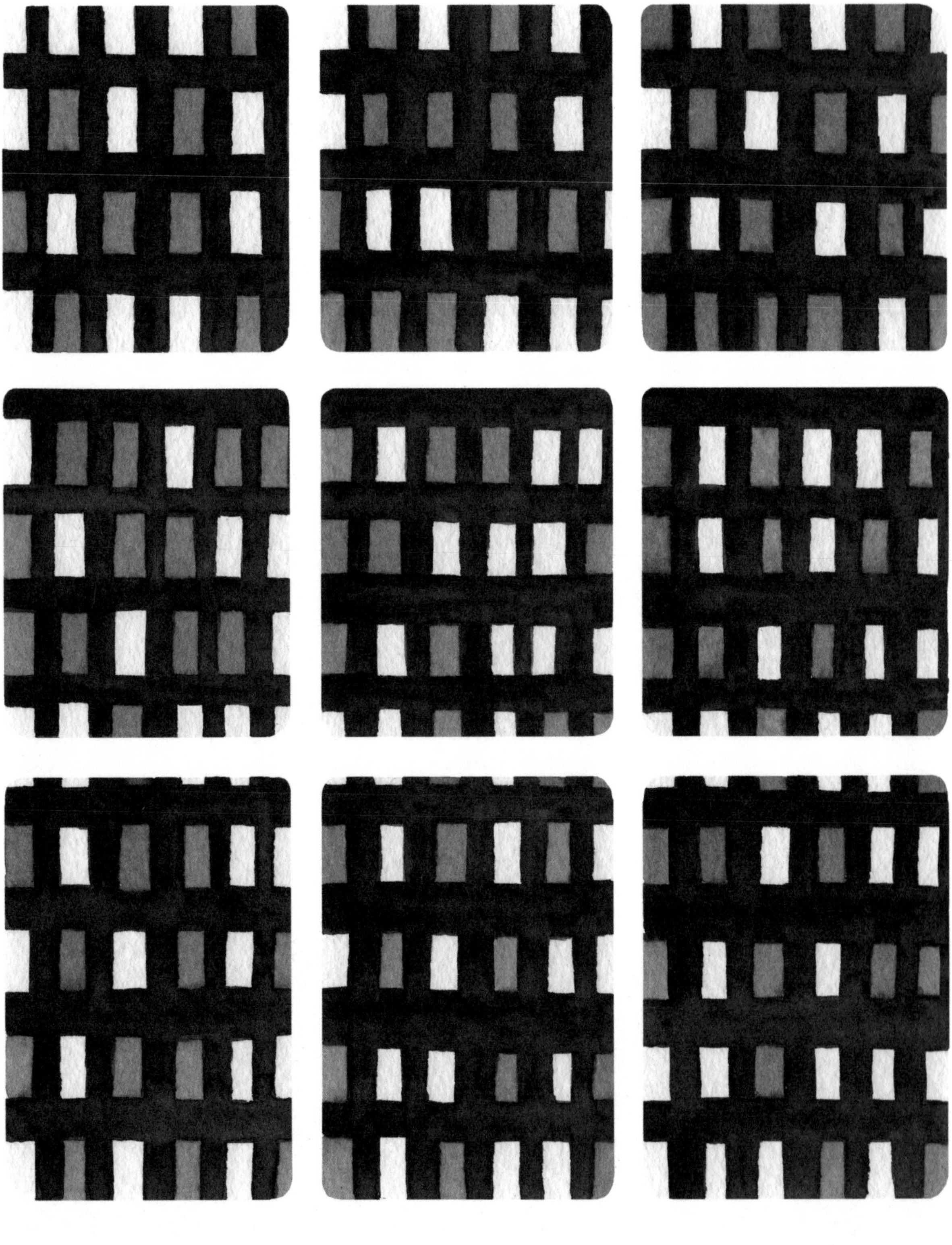

To witness the whole performance... you must stay awake until dawn.

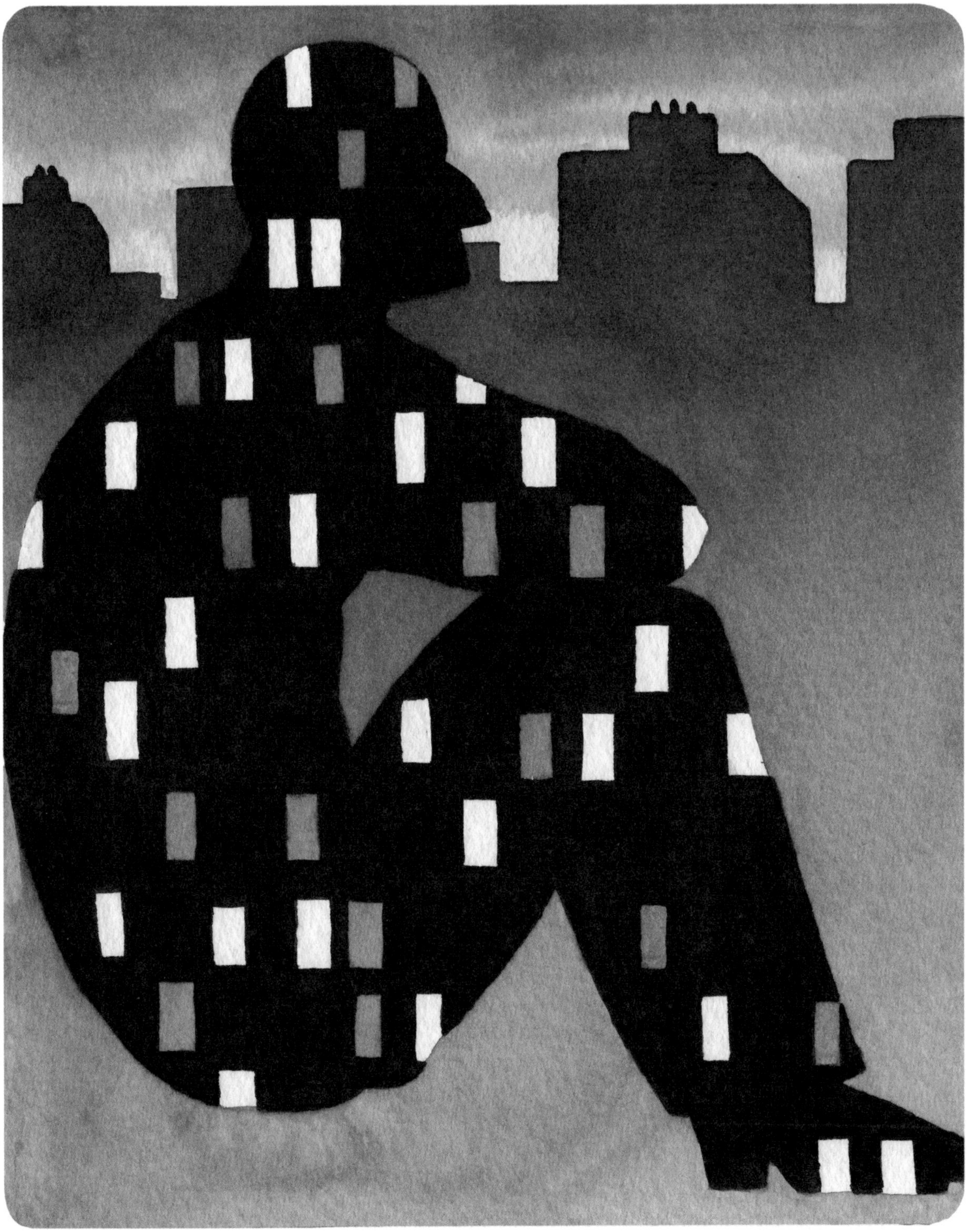

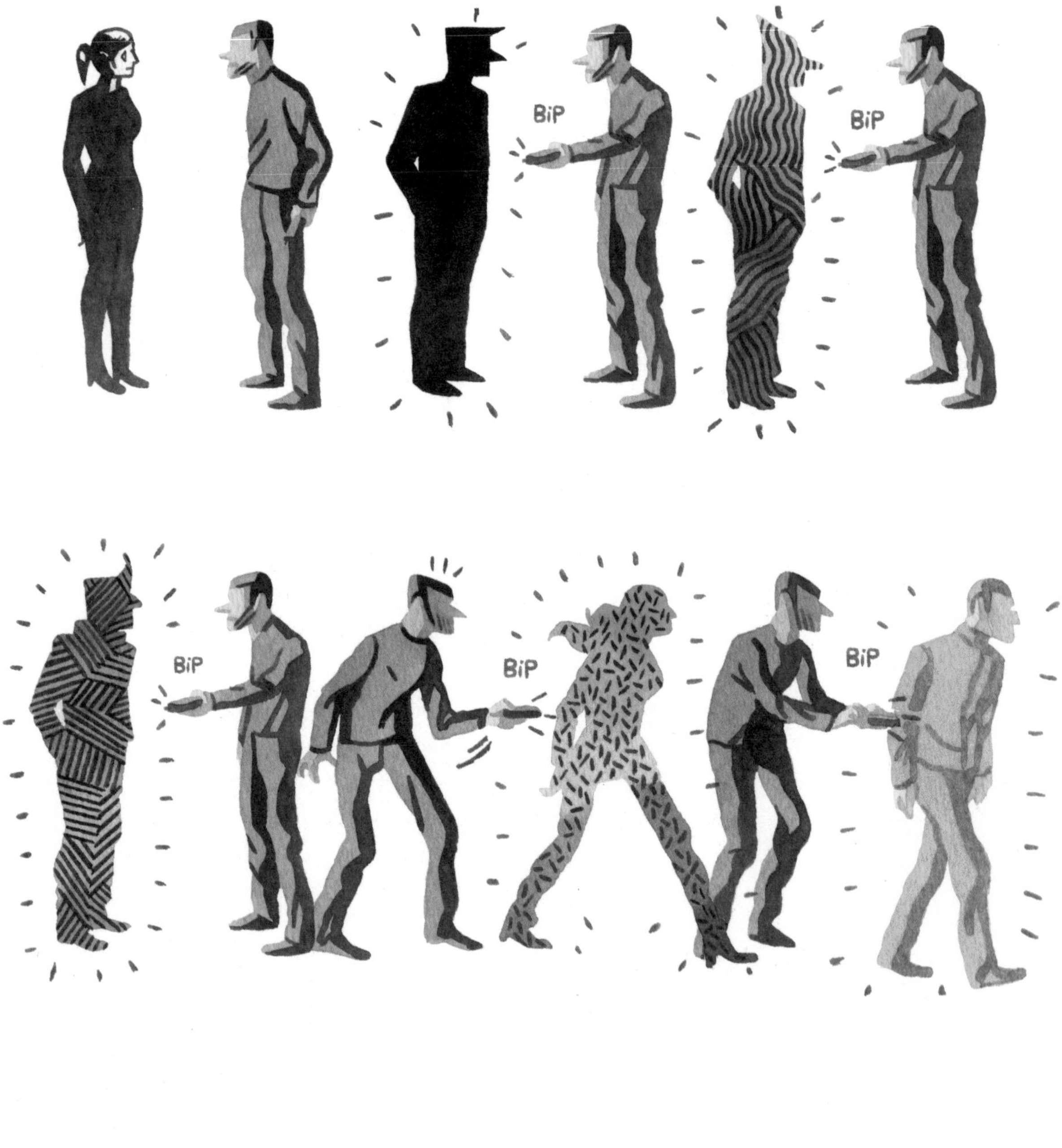
BiP
BiP
BiP
BiP
BiP

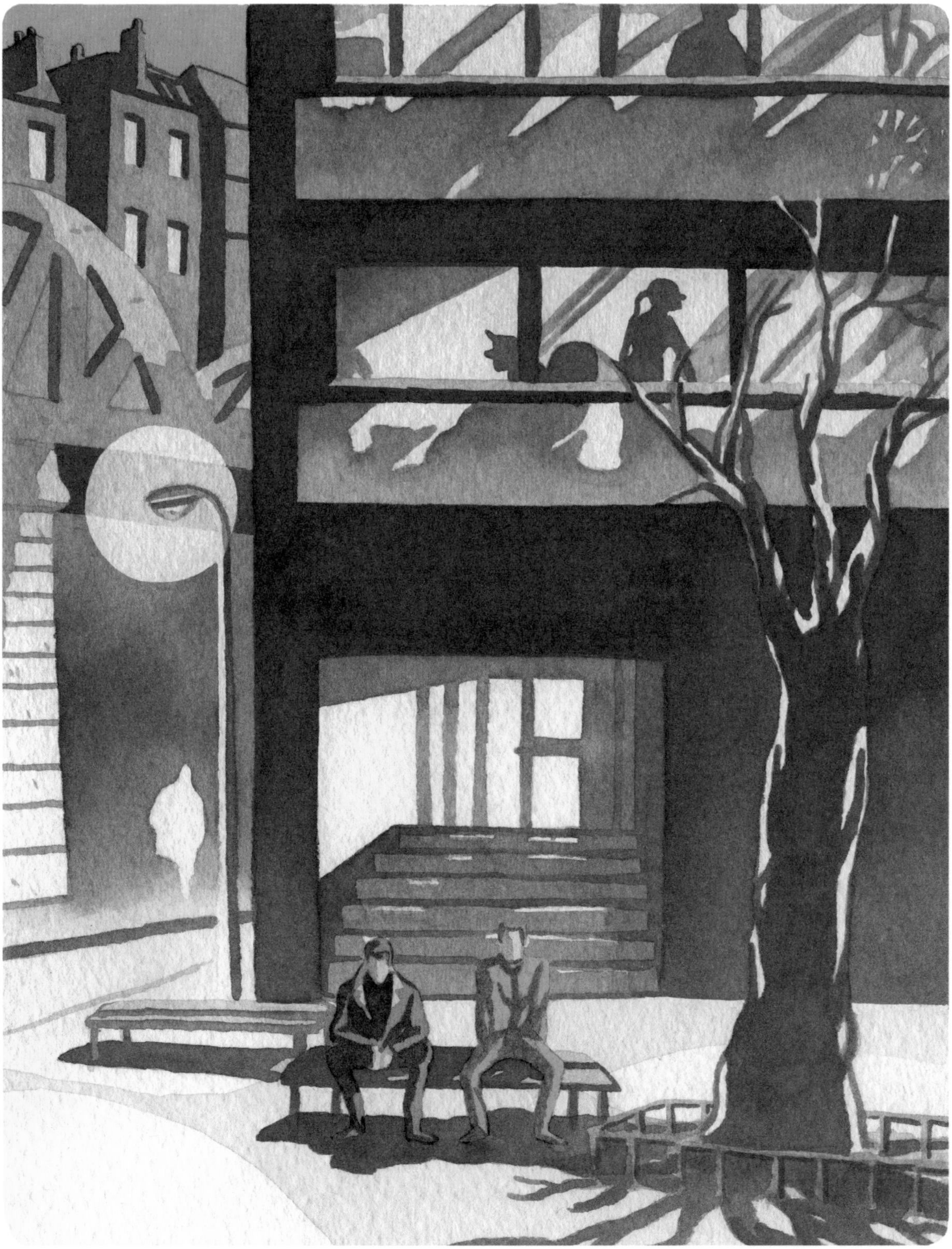

Two strangers look out over the city.

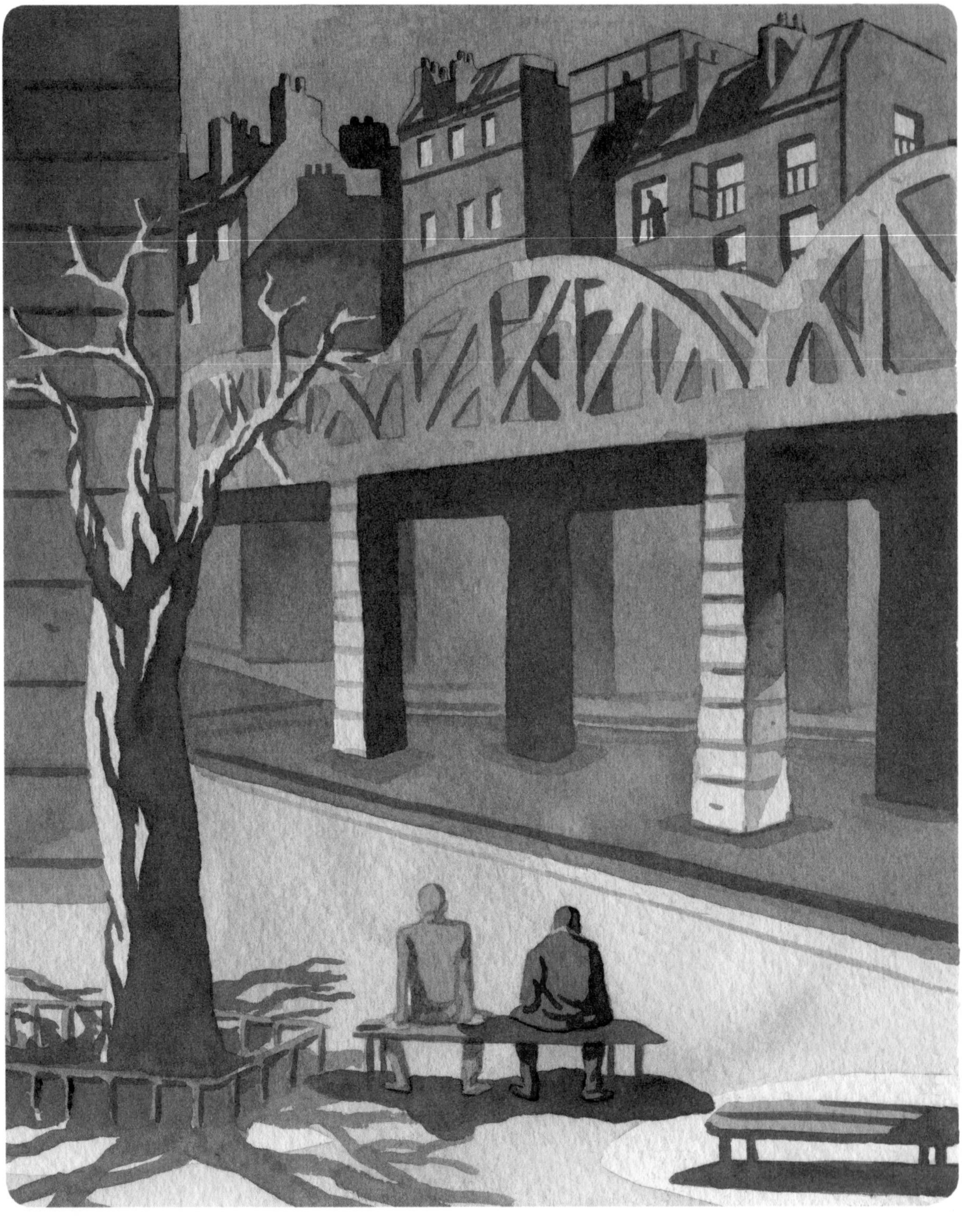

One observes the metro, the other directs his gaze to the rooftops.

They sit on a bench, a few centimetres separating them.
The landscape they see, therefore, is not exactly the same one.

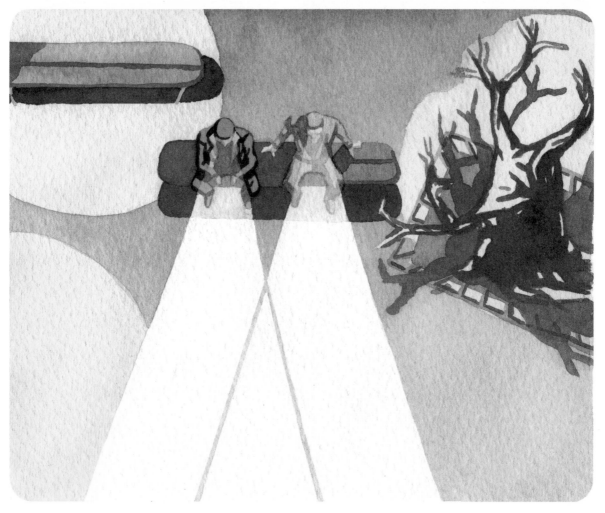

They don't realise it... but something profound closes the distance between them.

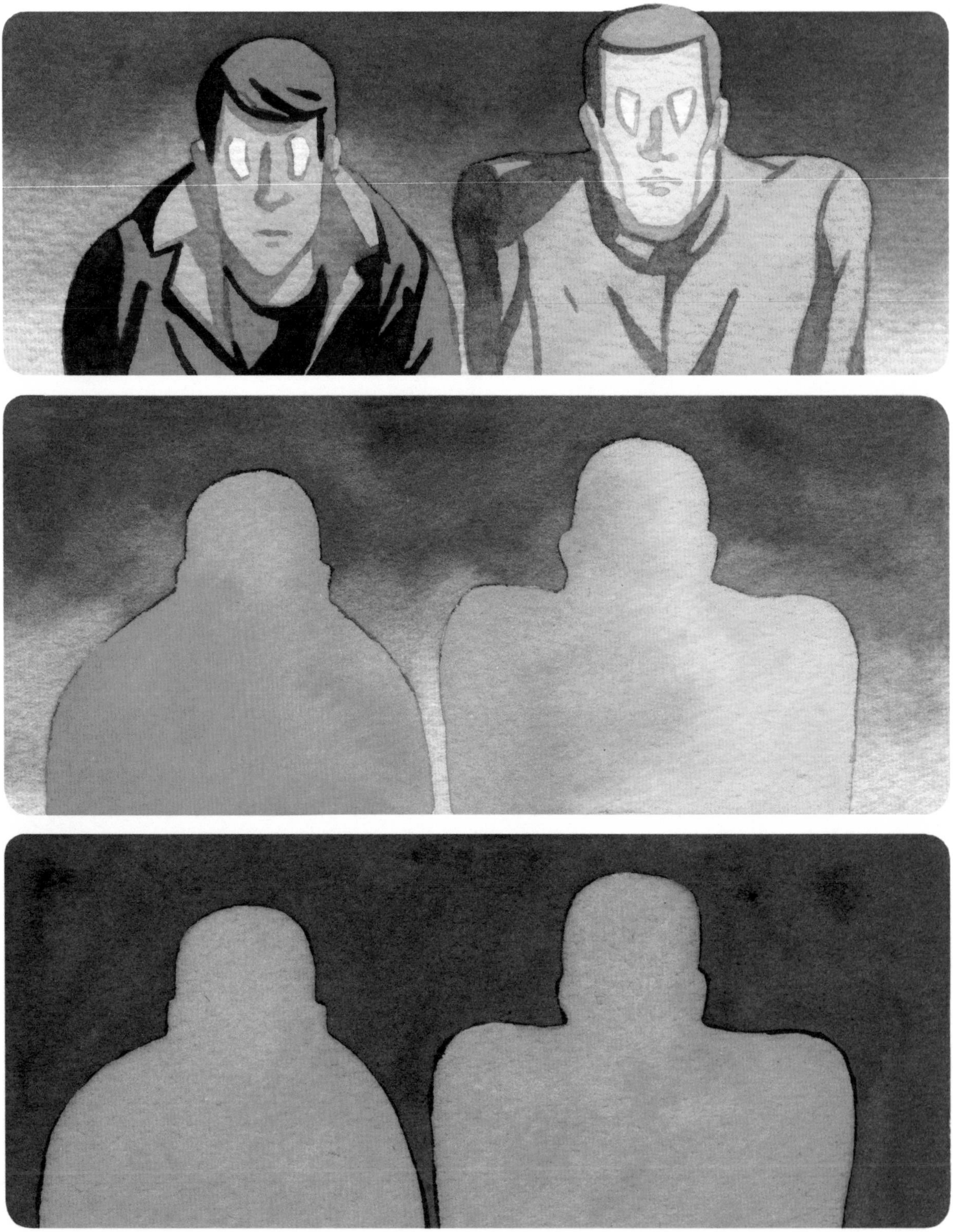

In their respective lifetimes, they have followed similar, though not identical, paths...

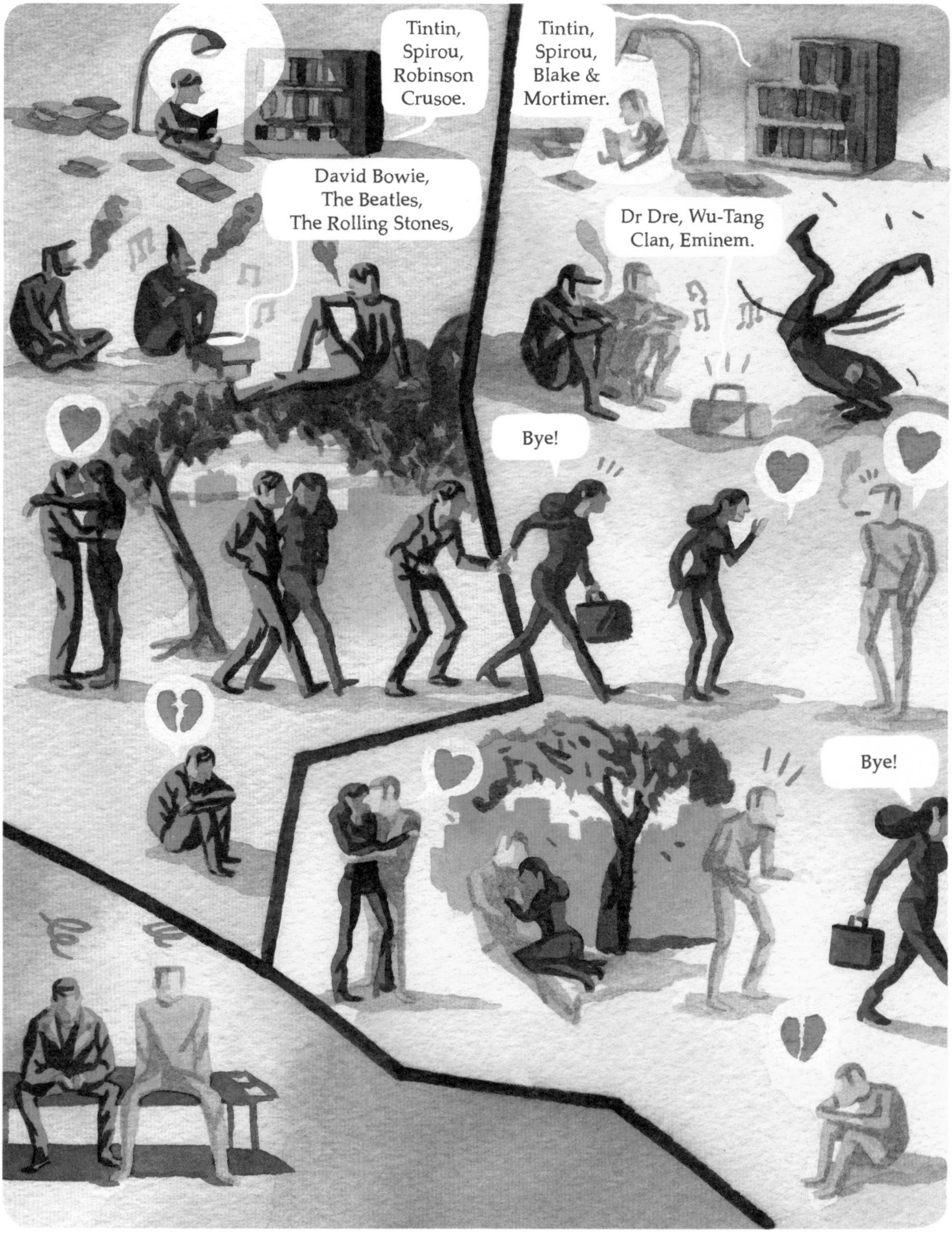
Tintin,
Spirou,
Robinson
Crusoe.
Tintin,
Spirou,
Blake &
Mortimer.
David Bowie,
The Beatles,
The Rolling Stones,
Dr Dre, Wu-Tang
Clan, Eminem.
Bye!
Bye!

Tonight, much like their lives, their perspectives are parallel....

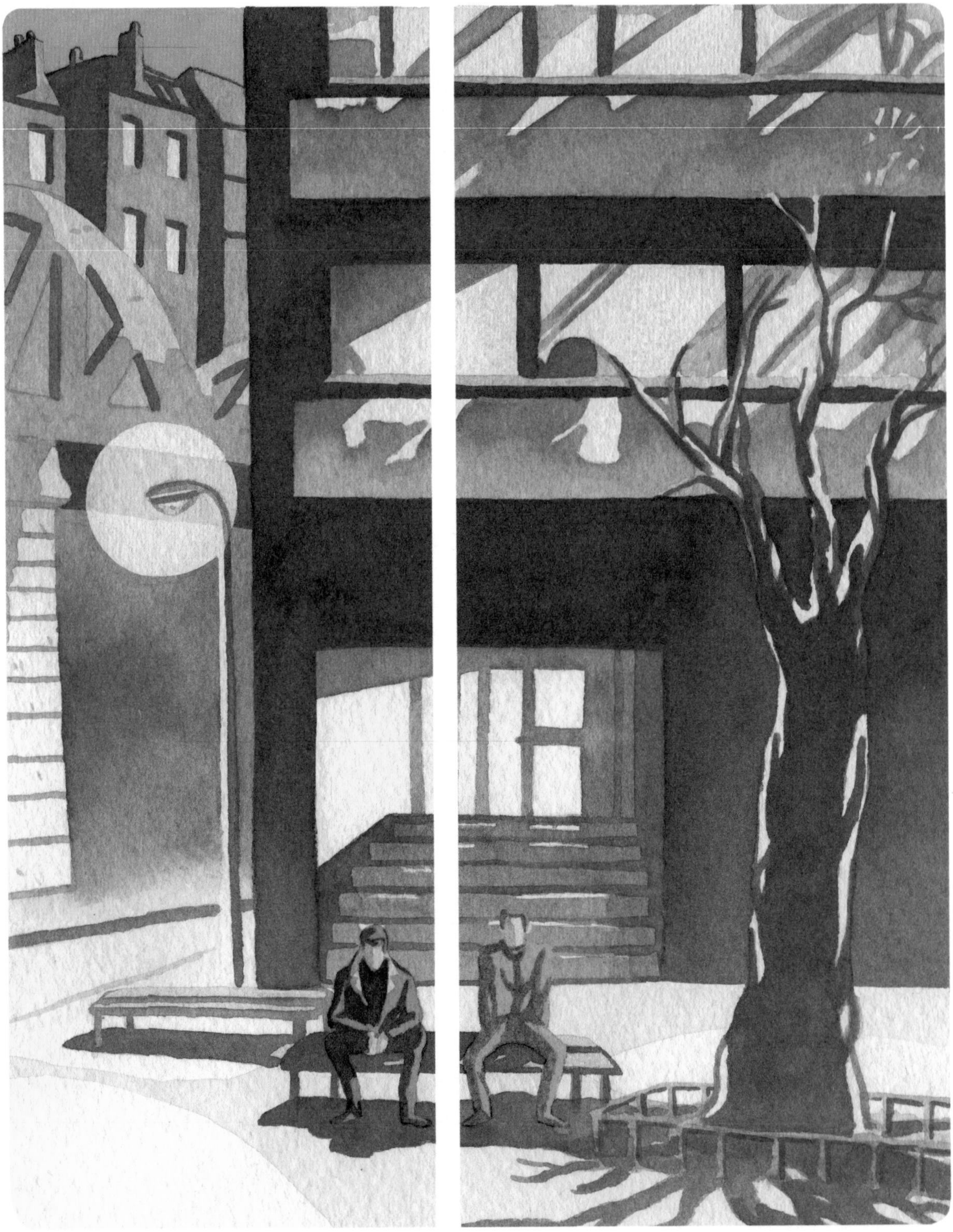

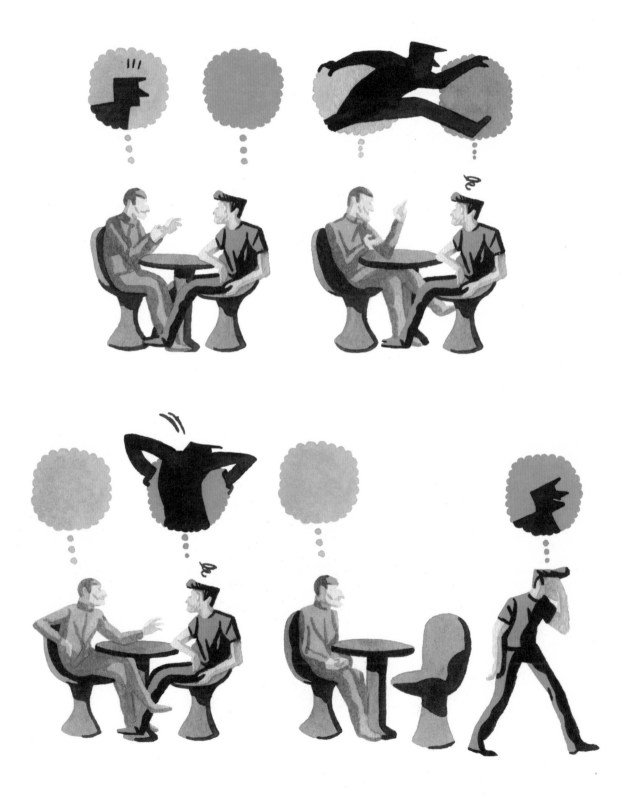

Arriving at a new station is as exciting as drawing a card in a poker game.

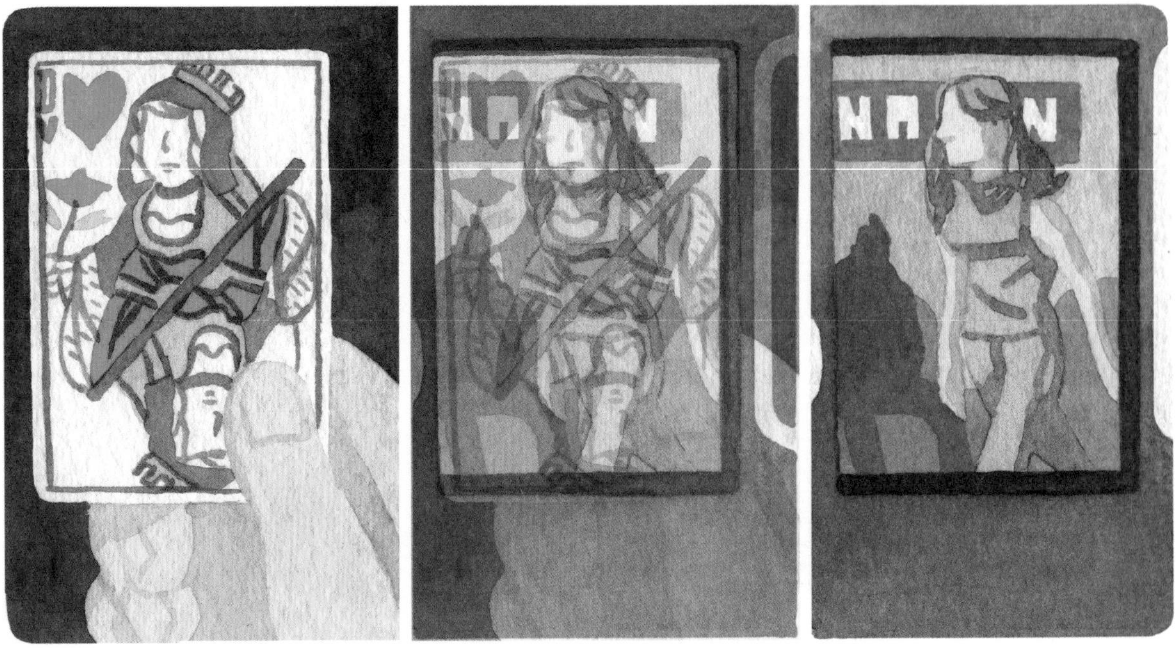

A new platform appears... it's a new deal of the cards...

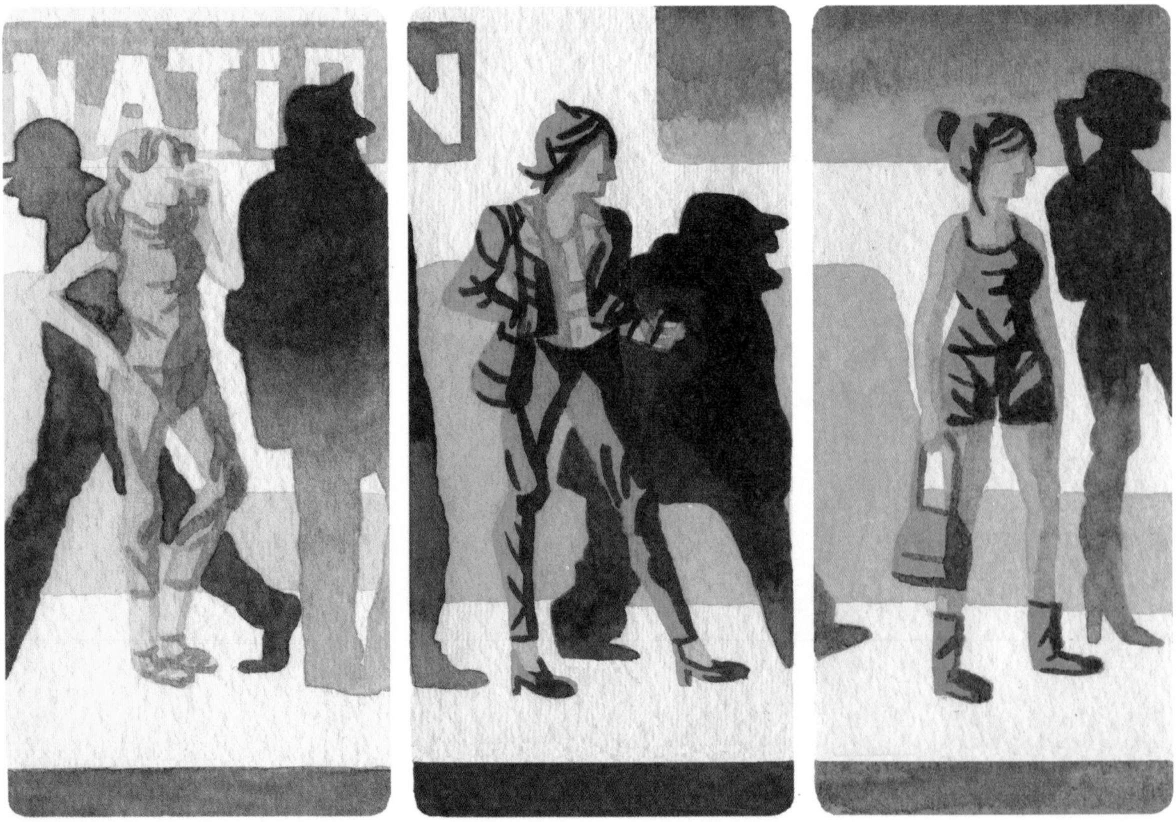

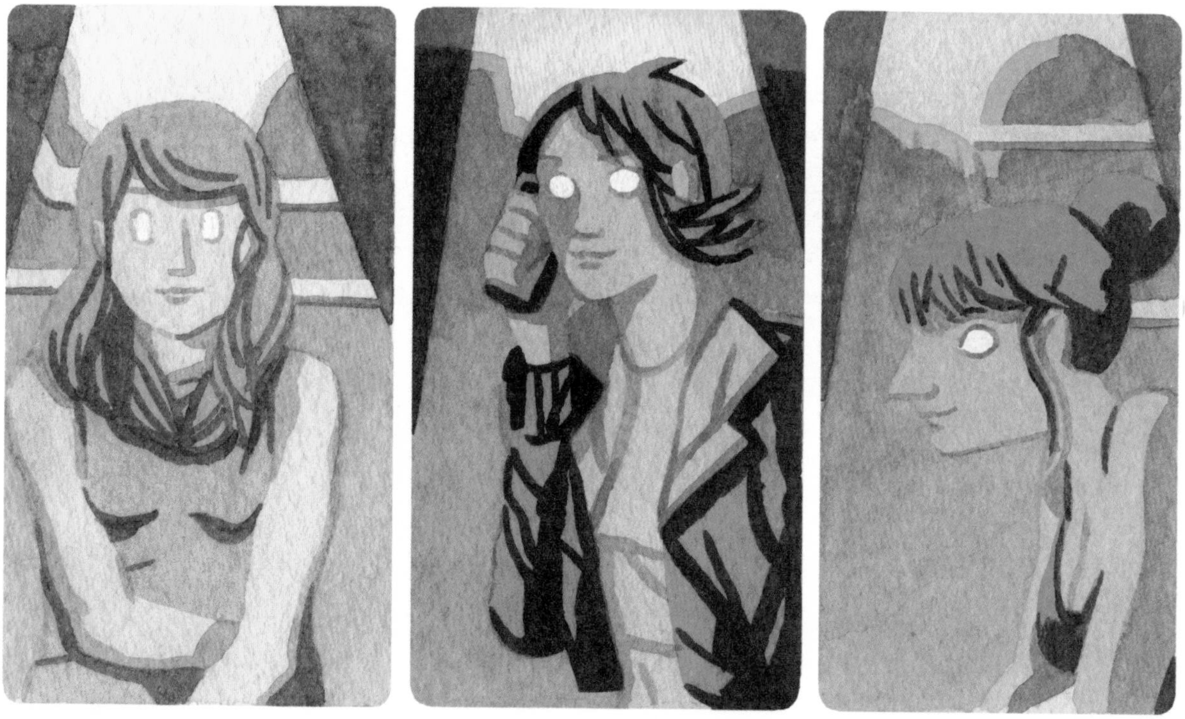

Some leave the game;

others join it...

but not always the ones you're expecting.

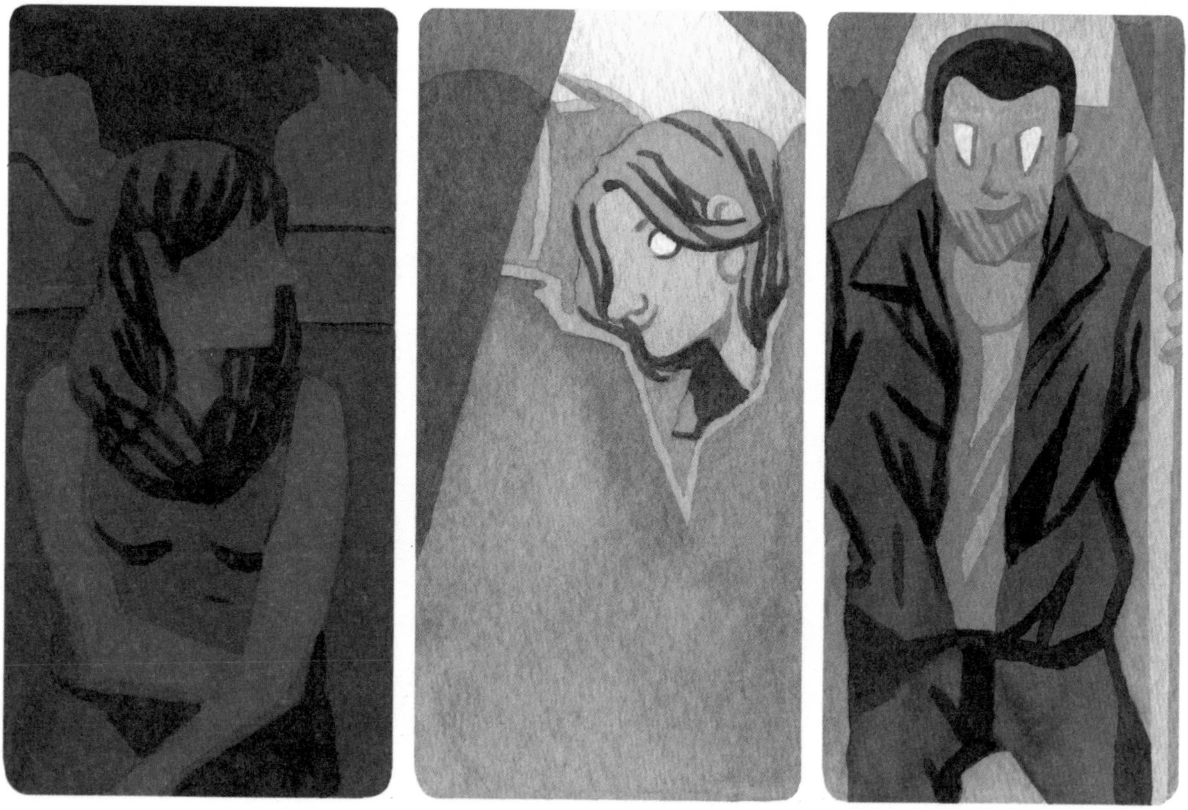

Each is full of promise, but is the one we really need still hidden in the deck?

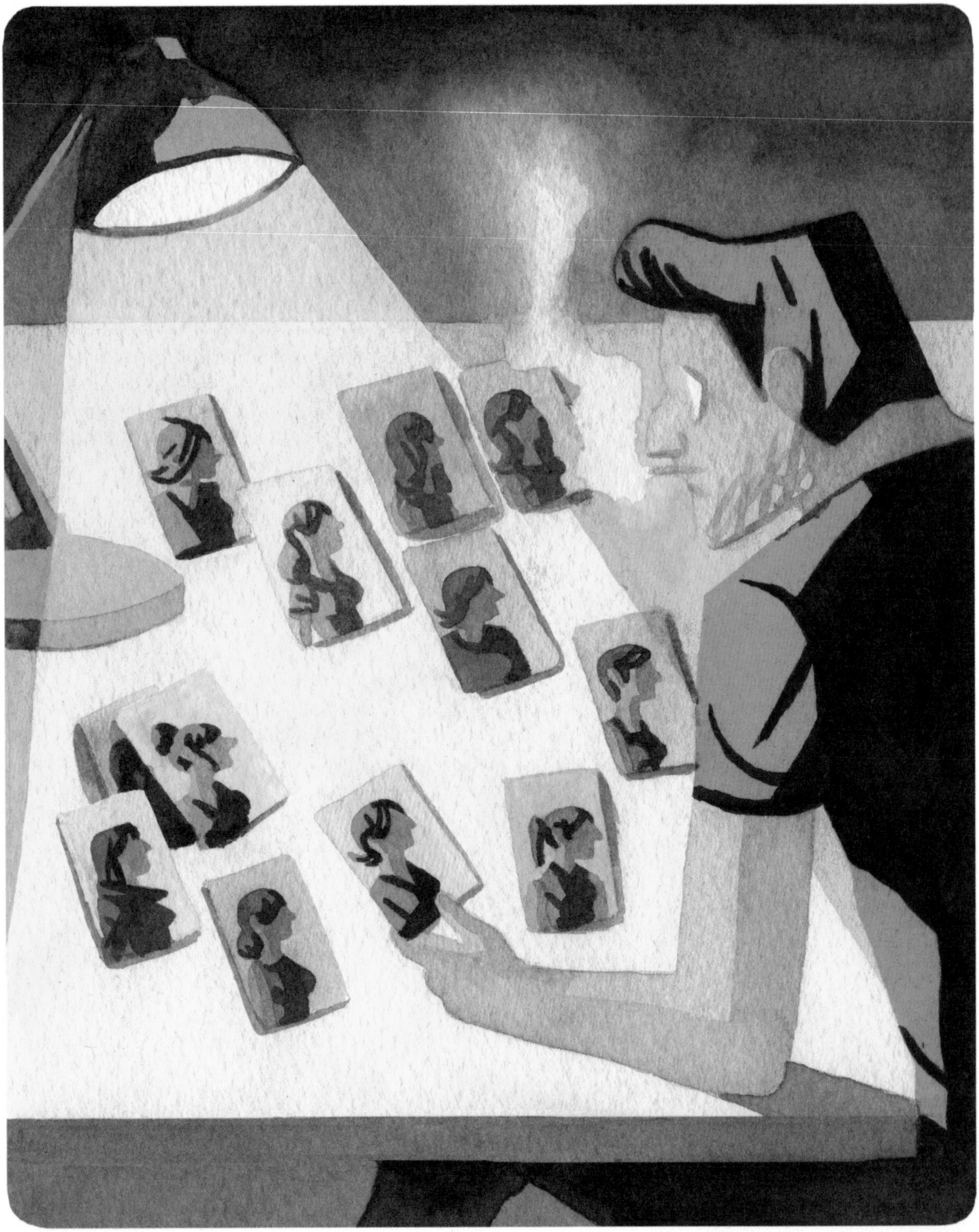

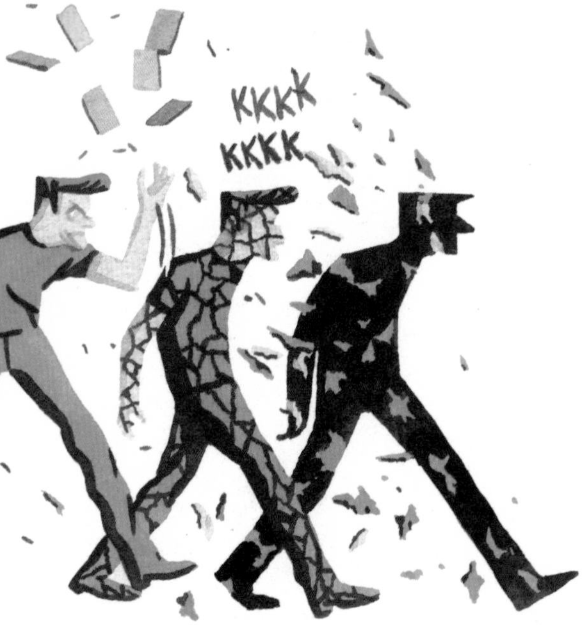
KKKK
KKKK

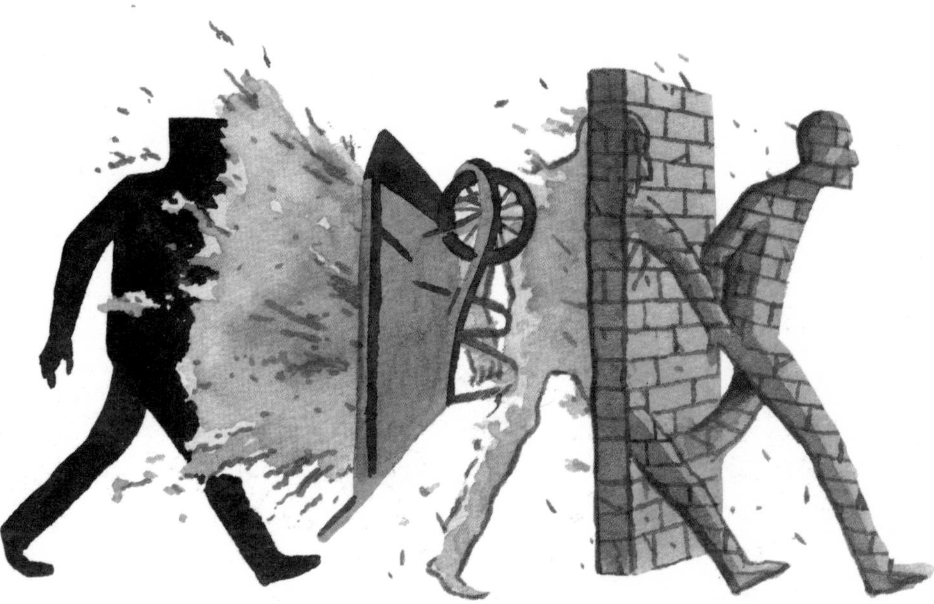

Measured against our lifetimes, the stuff of cities seems fixed and eternal...
But, being built by man, it too – like him – will perish in the end.

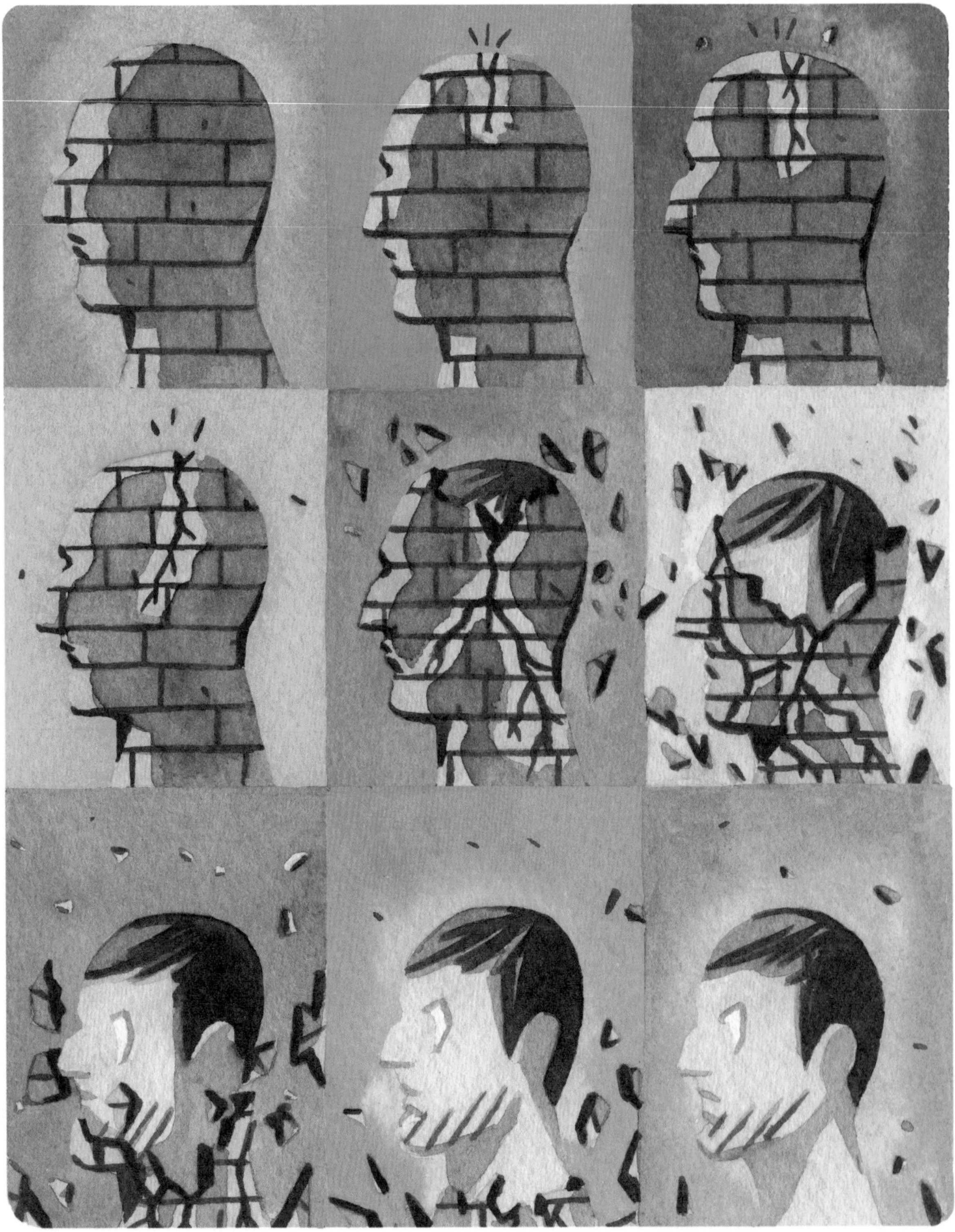

Measured against our lifetimes, all matter – whether living or inert – is a mirror.

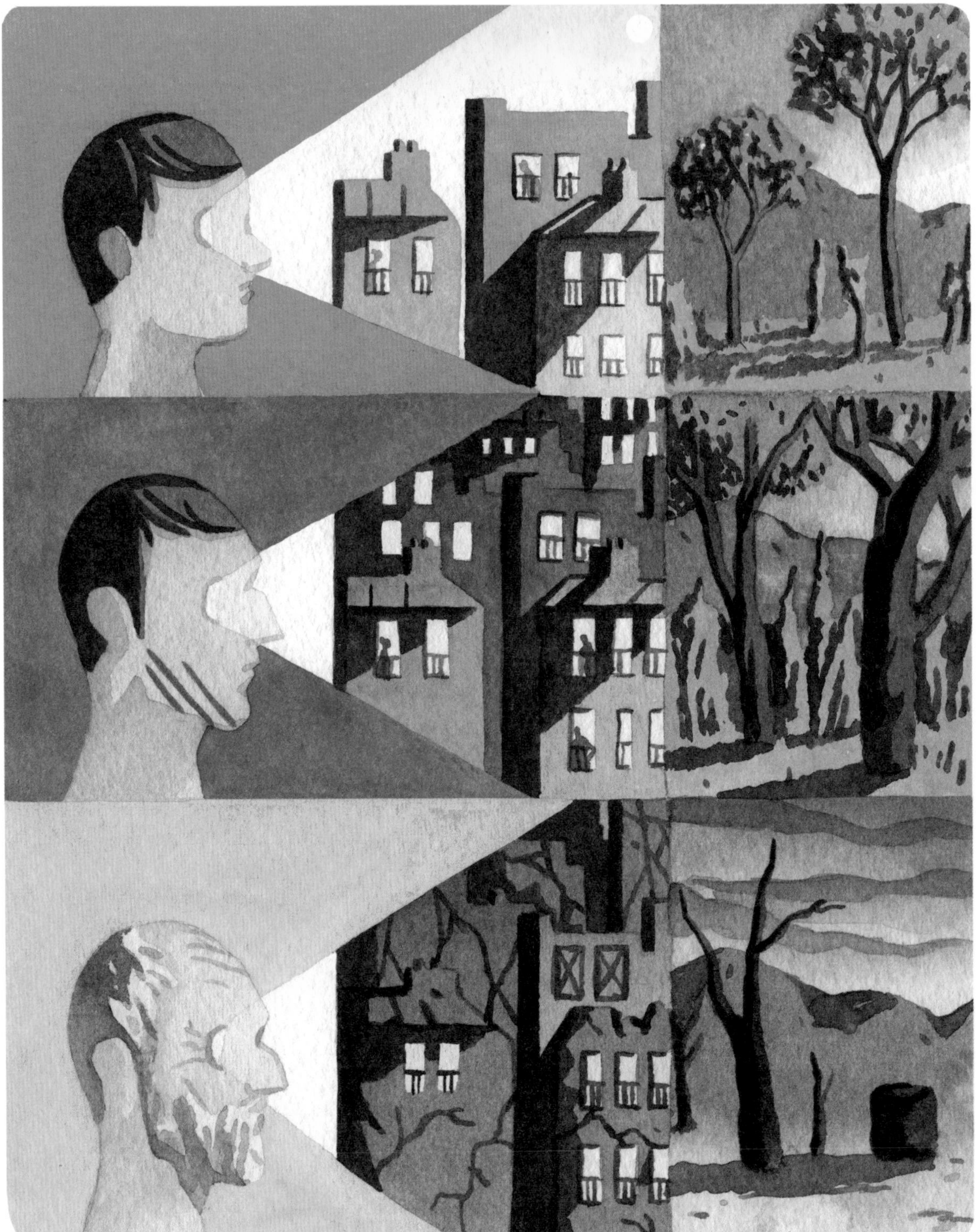

After each of us, it remains...

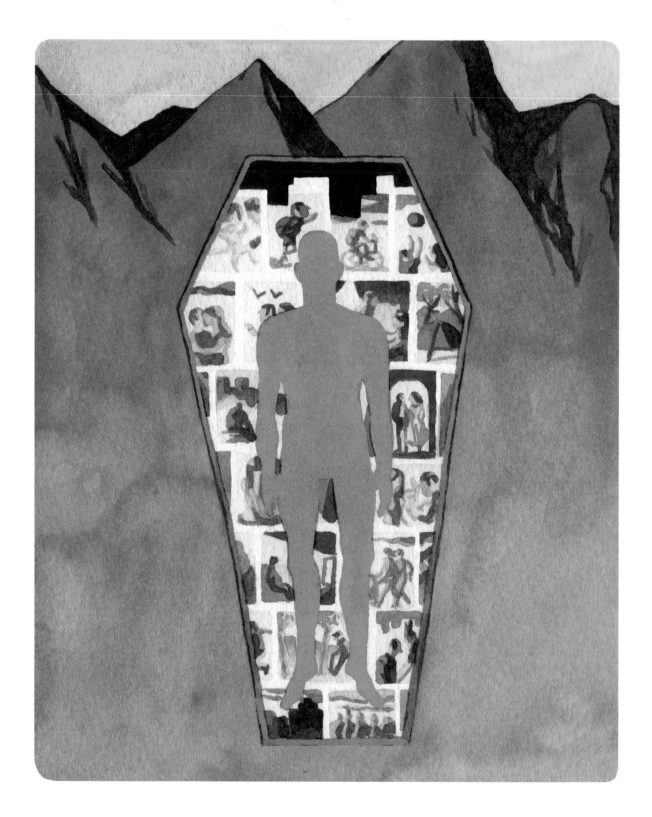

Man invents concepts to provide points of reference, to reassure himself...
imagining himself living in future generations...

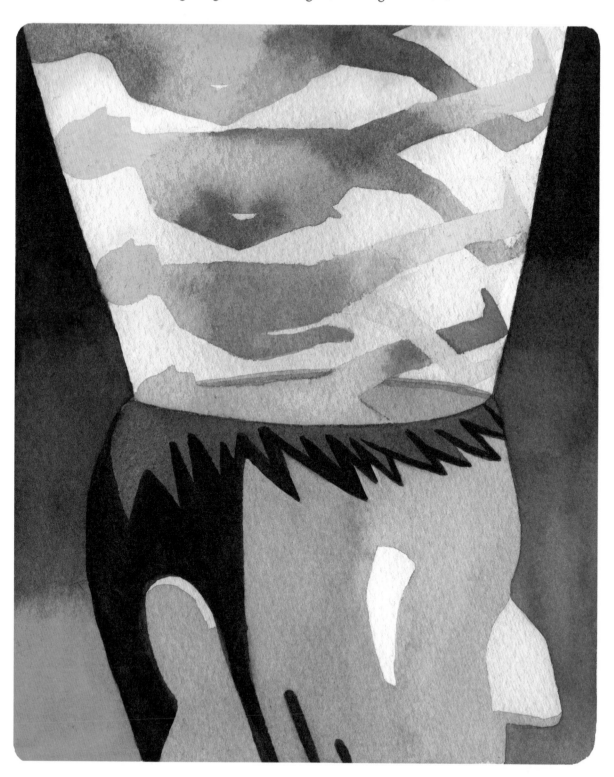

Hmm? This carriage... didn't I travel in it last week?

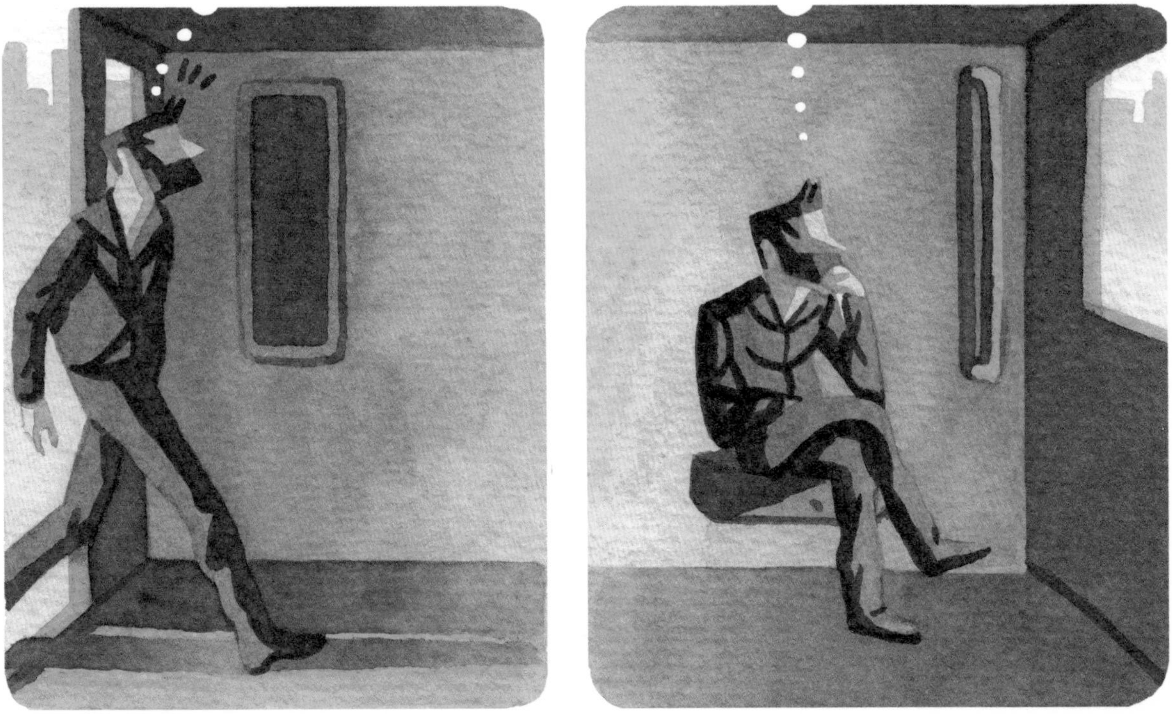

Or was it some time... long ago?

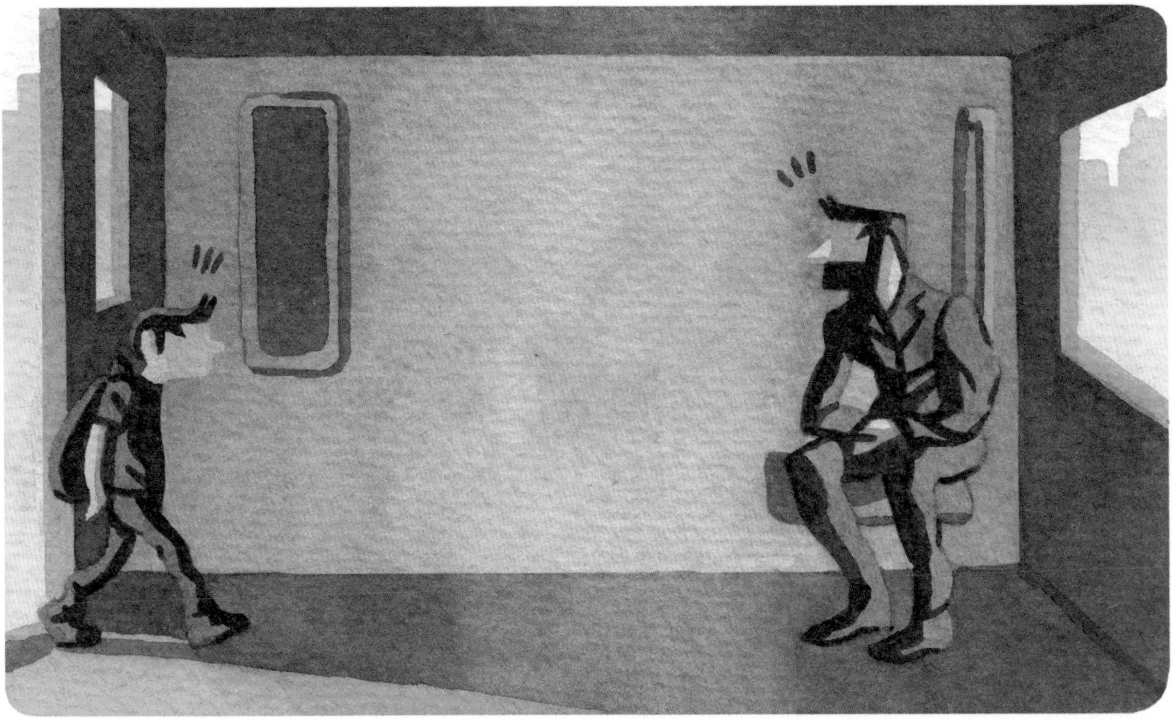

In a city square, an old man reminds me of someone I used to see there as a child...

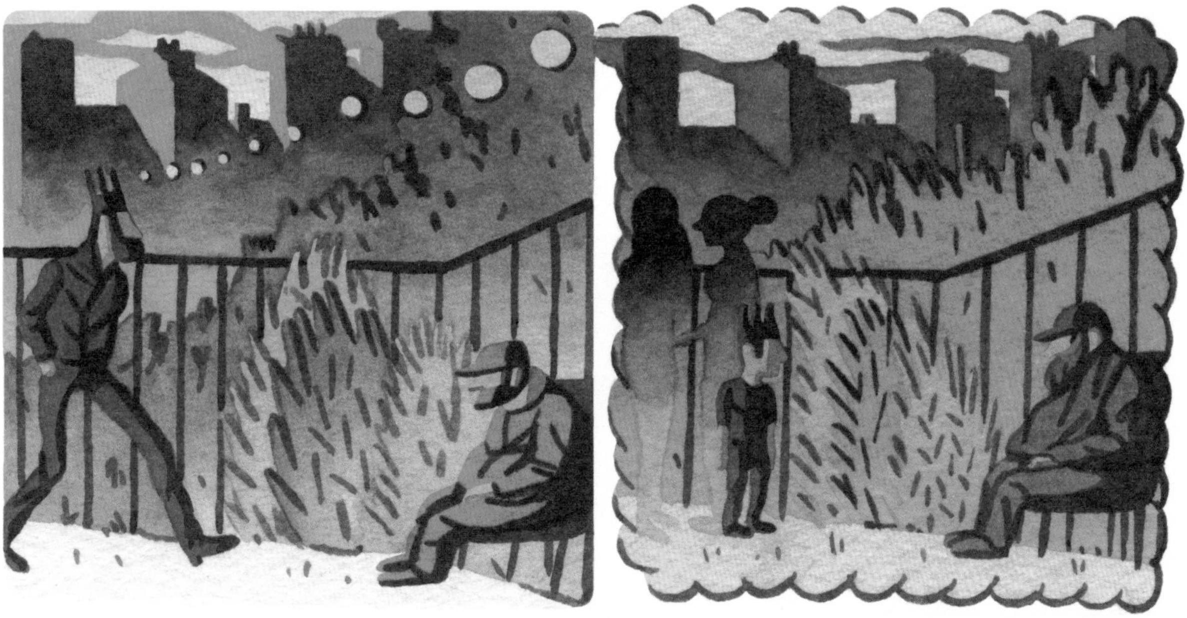

I could swear it's the same person...

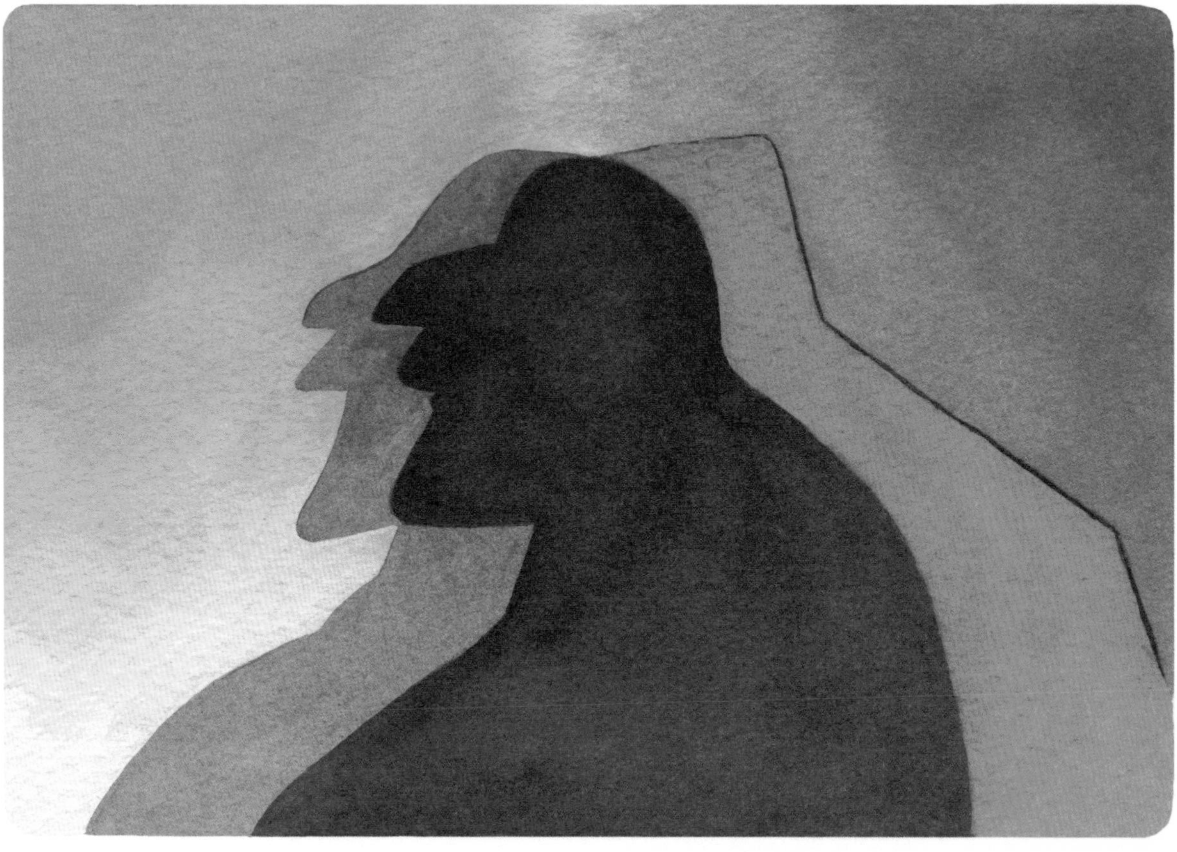

It's as if he's been here forever...

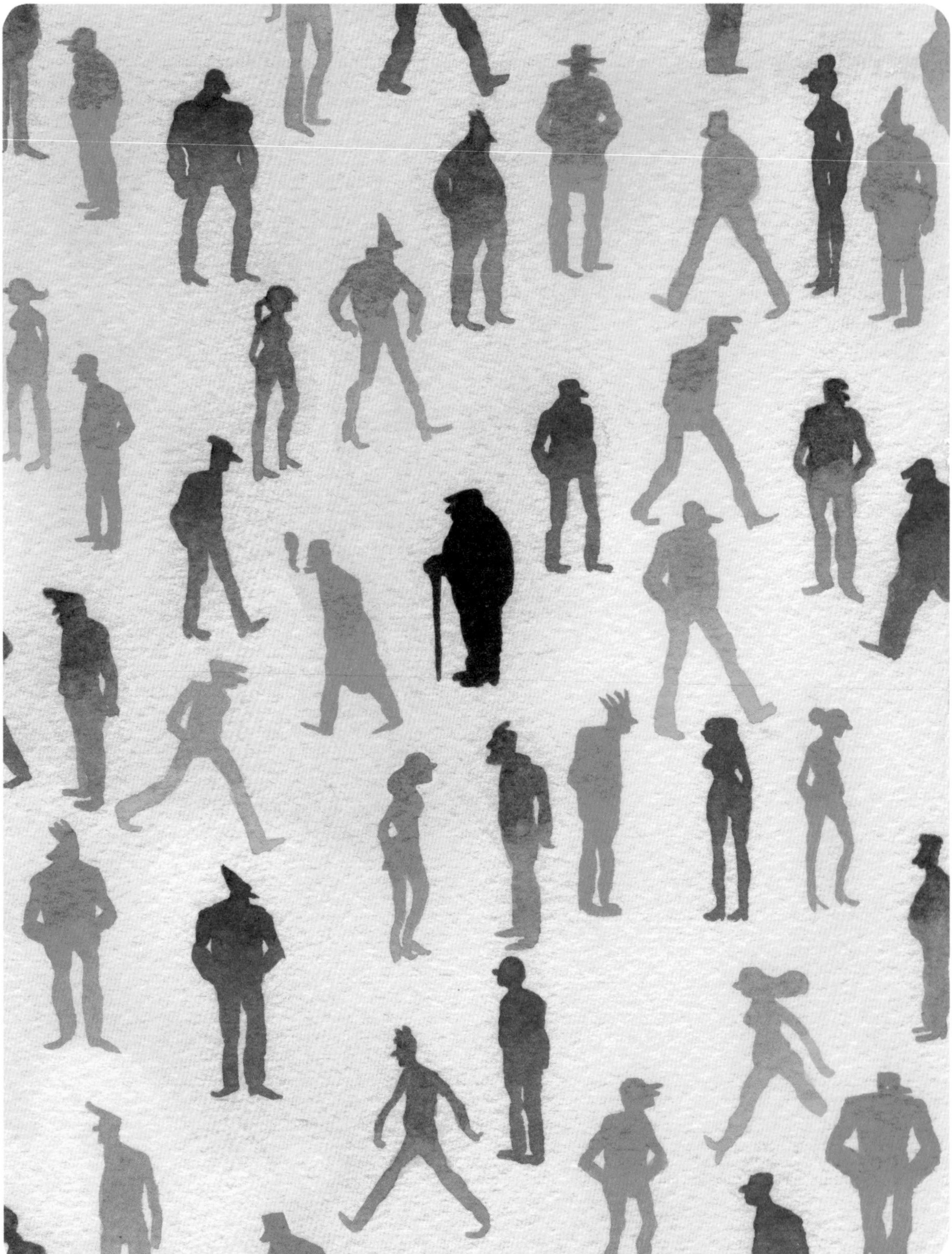

In each of our lives there are three stages: Childhood...

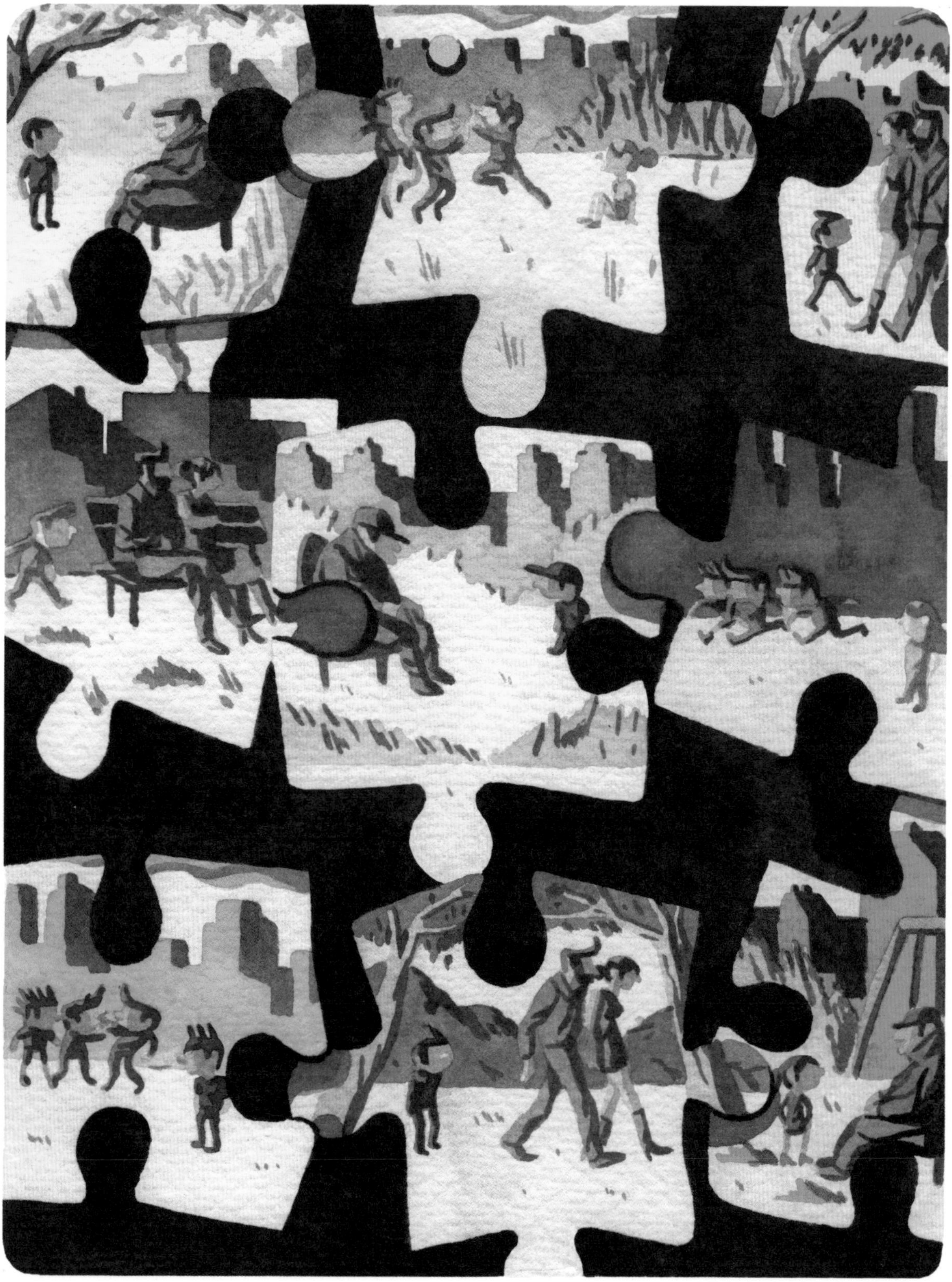

adulthood...

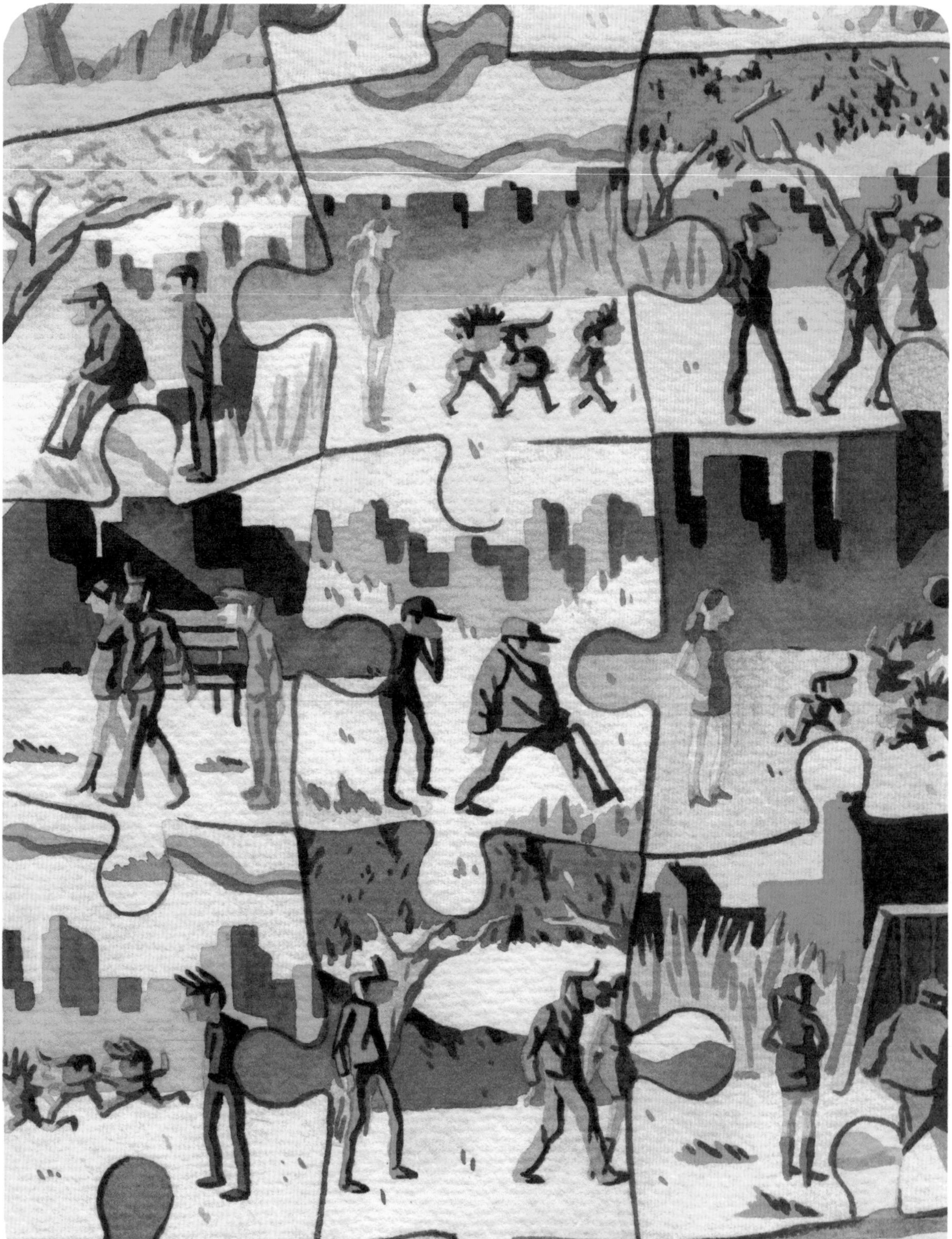

and old age...

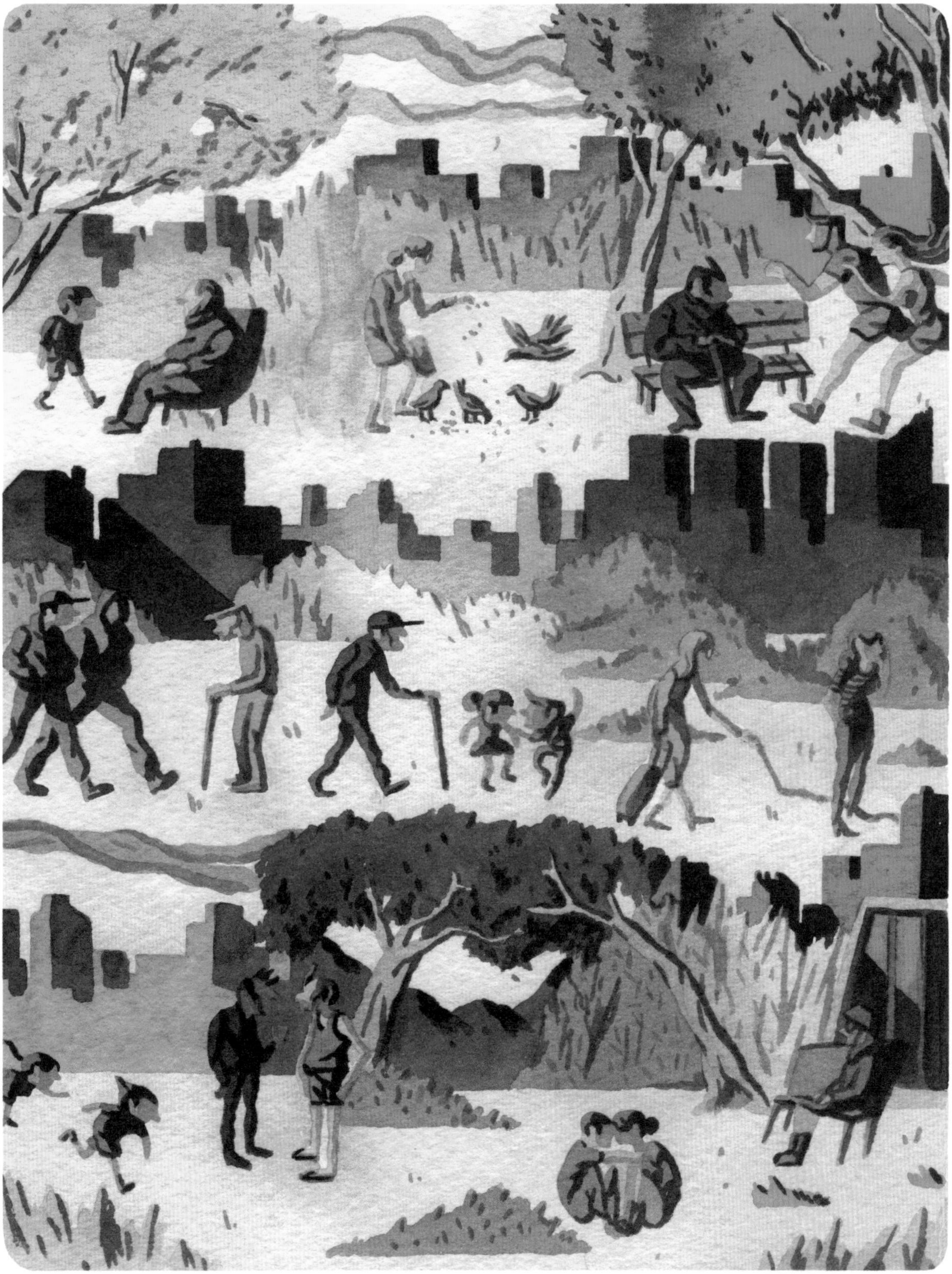

The ages of Man...

Each of us, in turn, will play these roles.

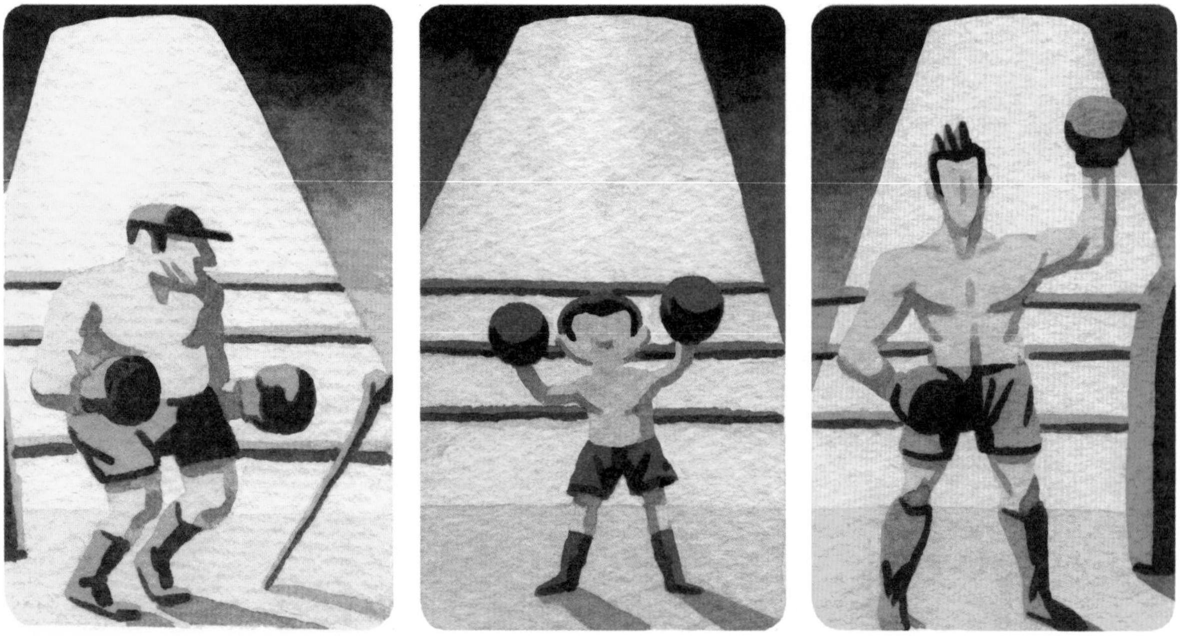

Only those closest to us – our friends and family – really change; we immediately notice the tiniest differences in them; they jump out at us; they disconcert us.

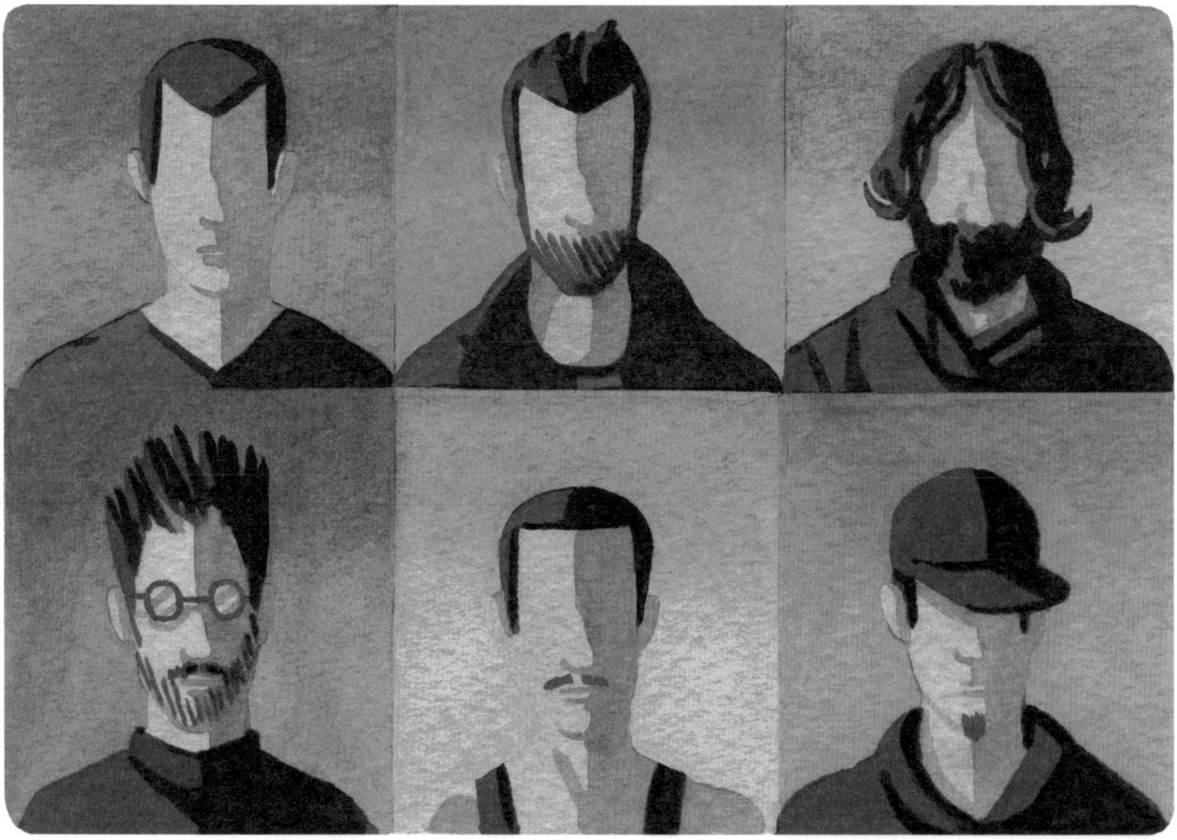

While the strangers we encounter in our lives, seem timeless, forever fixed in their roles.

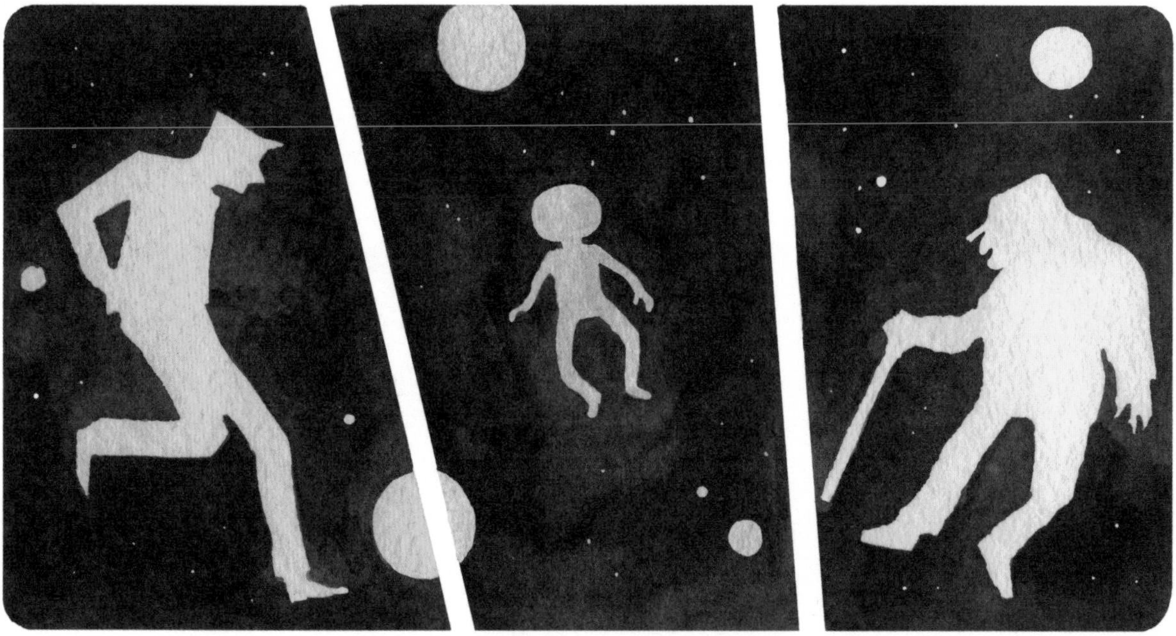

At the end of our own lives, we shouldn't be surprised
to find we have taken the place of the old man...

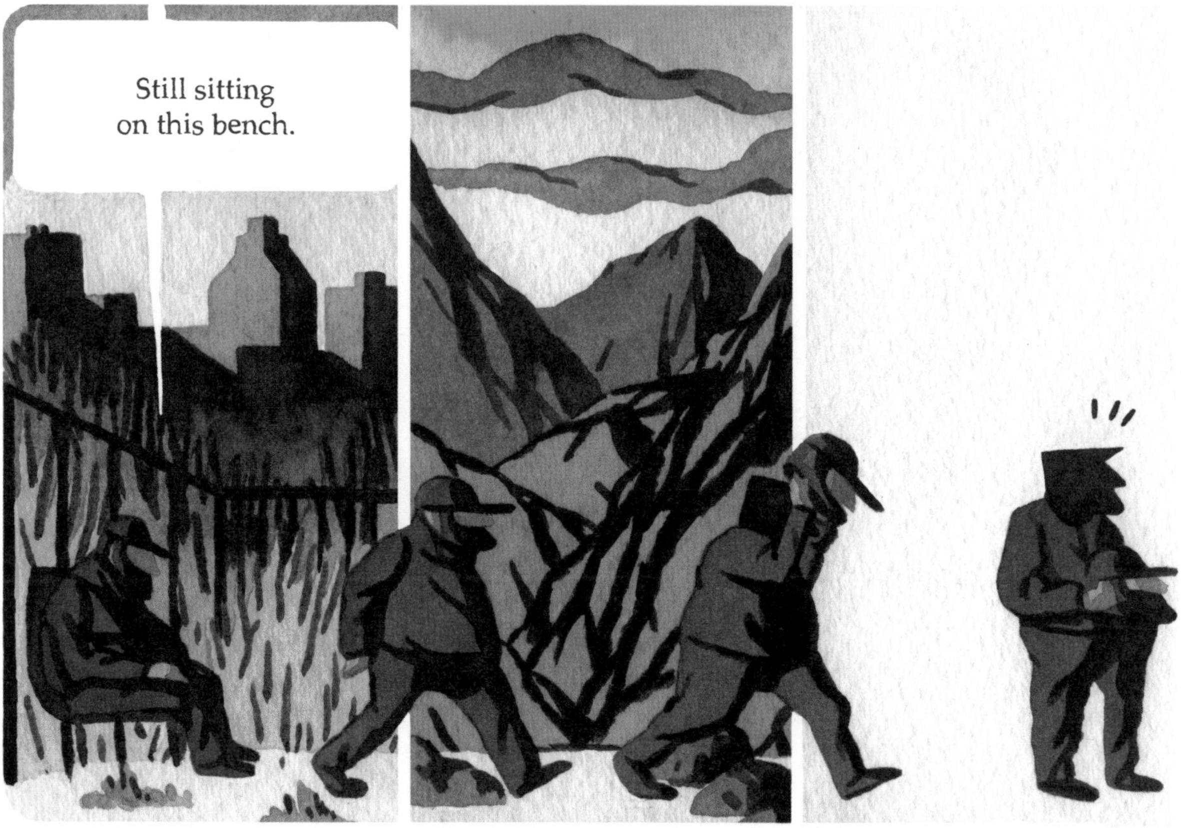
Still sitting on this bench.

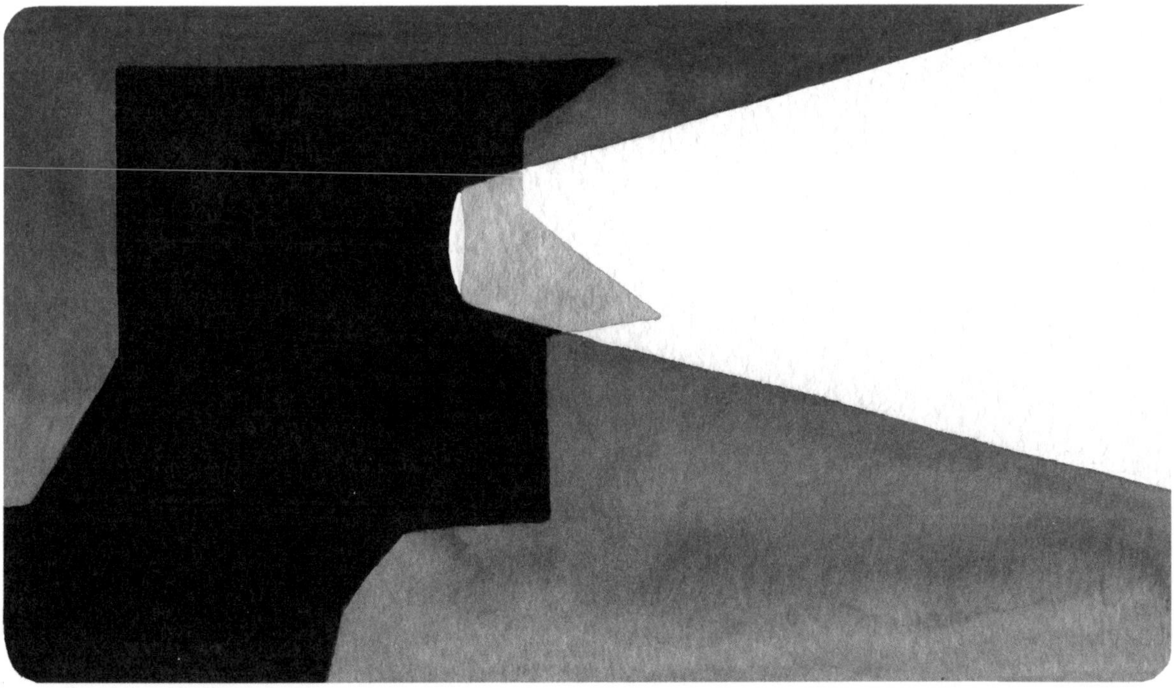

The Intelligence of Man continues to grow as the knowledge of each individual increases.

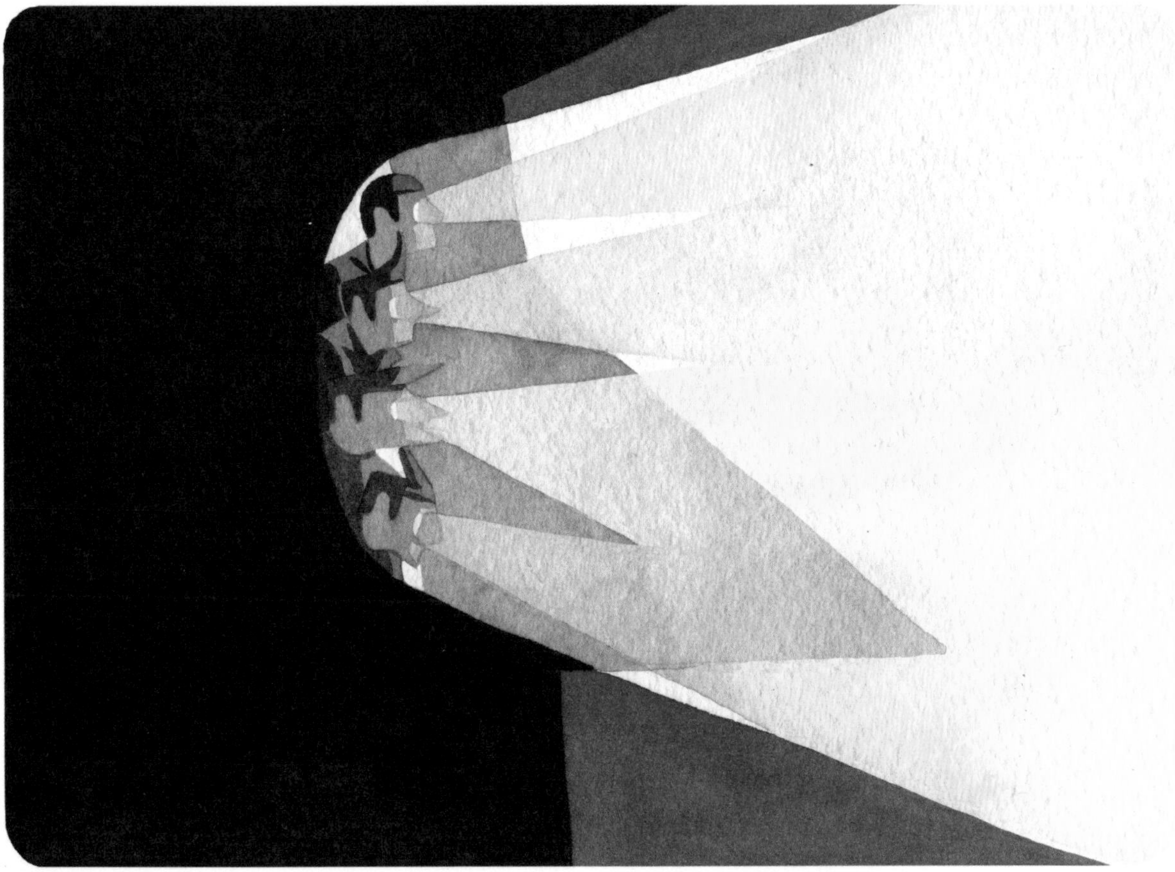

Their collective vision forms an expanding beam of light.

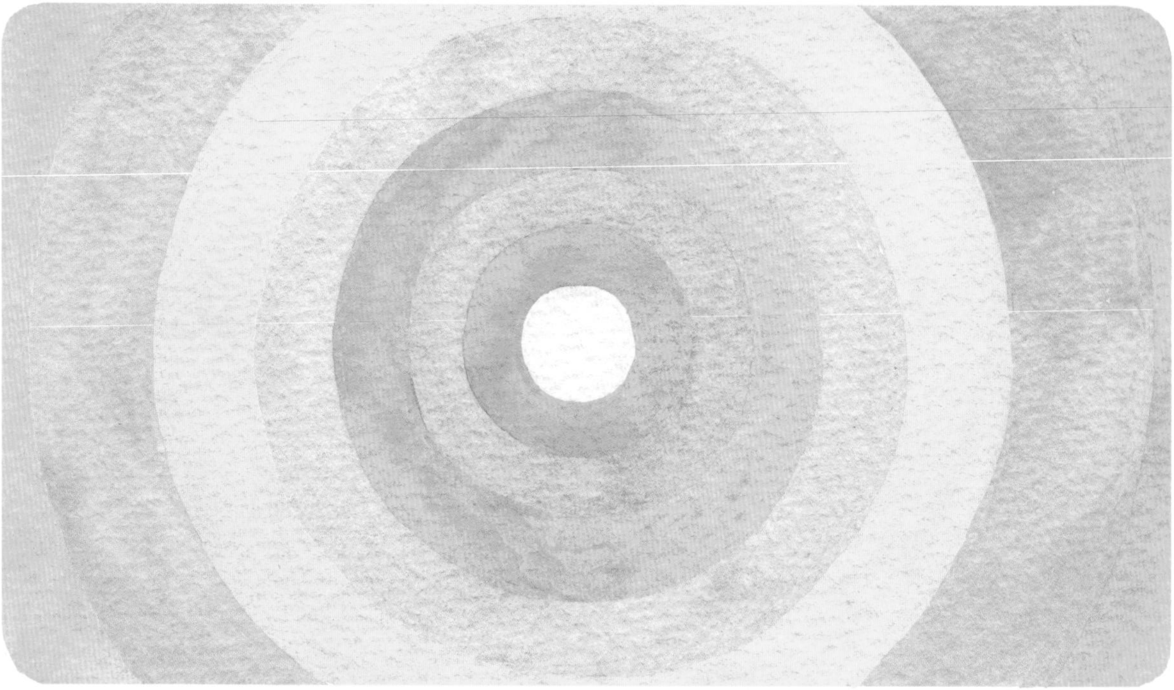

Man questions the world; it answers in riddles...

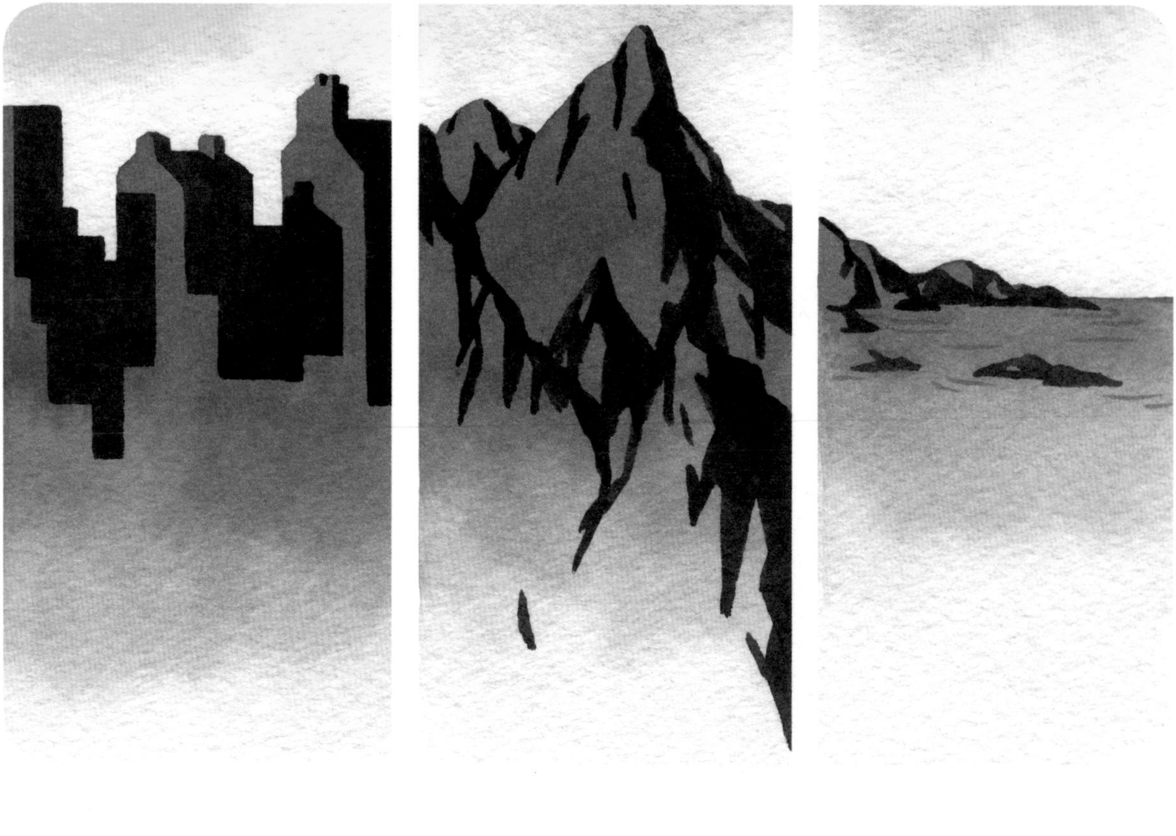

forcing him to continue searching for unattainable truths...

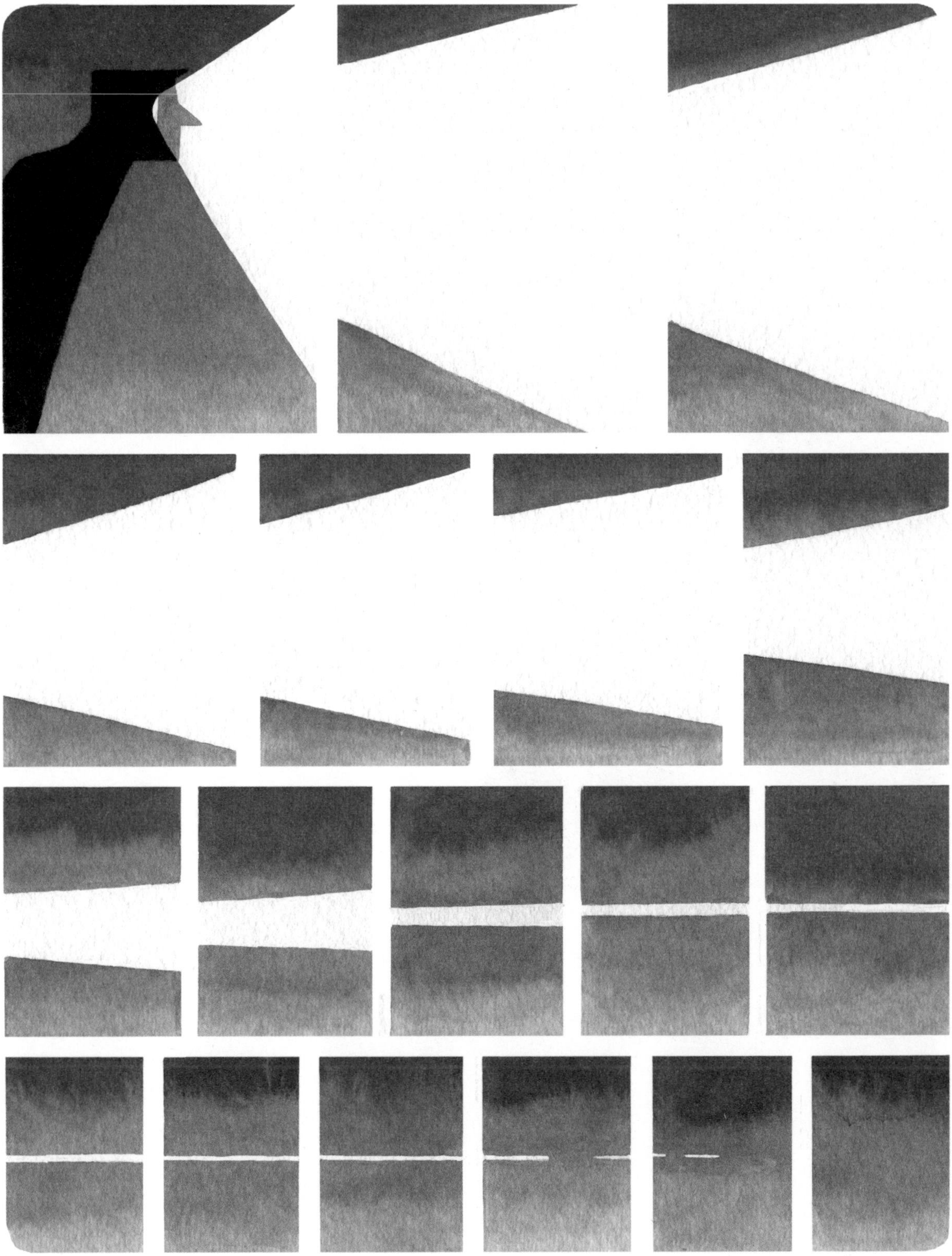

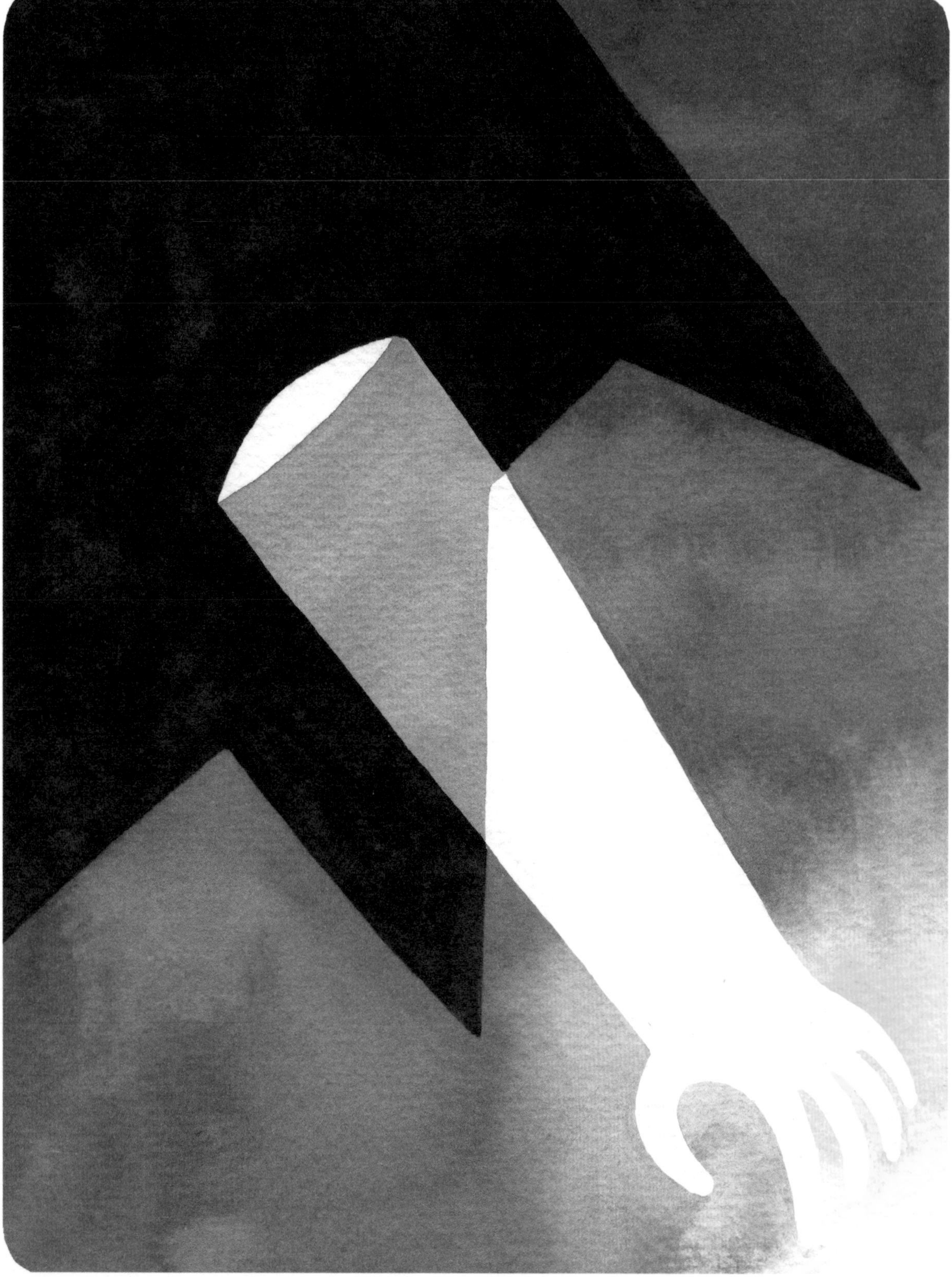

Maybe...

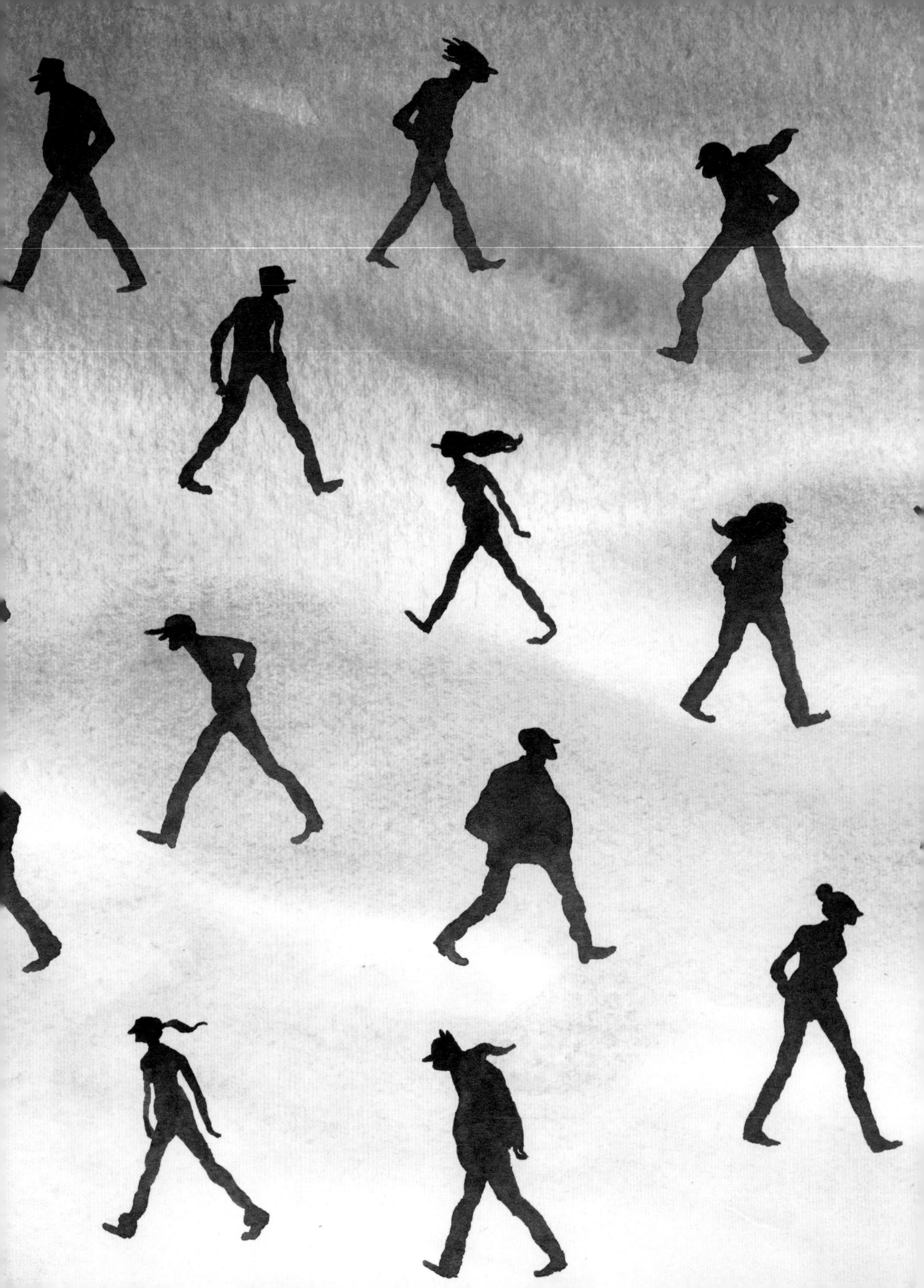